It's Not About the Burqa

Mariam Khan is a freelance writer and the editor of *It's Not About the Burqa*. She is also a contributor to the *Rife* anthology, edited by Nikesh Shukla. She's written for *Stylist*, *Metro*, *i-D*, *Dazed* and the *Guardian* on identity, feminism and politics.

'An incredibly important collection of essays that explores the pressures of being a Muslim woman today. These essays are passionate, angry, self-effacing, nuanced and utterly compelling in every single way'
                Nikesh Shukla, editor of *The Good Immigrant*

'Wide-ranging . . . engrossing . . . fascinating . . . these essays take a courageous and panoramic view of Muslims'
                                                Observer

'A landmark anthology . . . frank and engaging essays on sex and religion, mental health in the Muslim community and queer identity from an impressive selection of writers and activists'   *Cosmopolitan*

'Essential reading for our times. These essays are funny, angry, hopeful, sorrowful and inspired – and will leave you feeling much the same'
                        Kiran Millwood Hargrave, author of
                                The Girl of Ink and Stars

'An intelligent and much-needed book'   *Red*

'It's about pushing past the stereotype placed on Muslim women and hearing the individuals themselves; it's required reading'   *Stylist*

'Refreshing and badass'   *Metro*

'*It's Not About the Burqa* is a valuable book, fulfilling its aim of giving Muslim women a space of their own'
                        Sarah Shaffi, *The New Arab*

'Seventeen brilliantly wide-ranging essays covering everything from the rise of the sexualized Islamic influencer, to the Quran's take on bisexuality – and of course insidious, ugly Islamophobia'   *i*

Edited by Mariam Khan

IT'S
NOT
ABOUT
THE
BURQA

Muslim Women on Faith, Feminism,
Sexuality and Race

PICADOR

First published 2019 by Picador

First published in paperback 2020 by Picador

This paperback edition first published 2020 by Picador
an imprint of Pan Macmillan
The Smithson, 6 Briset Street, London EC1M 5NR
Associated companies throughout the world
www.panmacmillan.com

ISBN 978-1-5098-8642-5

Typeset in Stempel Garamond by Jouve (UK), Milton Keynes
Printed and bound by CPI Group (UK) Ltd, Croydon, CR0 4YY

MIX
Paper from
responsible sources
FSC® C116313

Visit www.picador.com to read more about all our books
and to buy them. You will also find features, author interviews and
news of any author events, and you can sign up for e-newsletters
so that you're always first to hear about our new releases.

To Amelia and Elah.

Contents

Glossary

abaya – robe-like dress or cloak
alhamdullilah – all praise and thanks be to Allah
burqa – outer garment covering the body and face,
   with a mesh grille or window across the eyes
chappals – sandals, usually made of leather
desi – the people and culture of South Asia and their
   diaspora
dua – prayer
dhoti – a piece of cloth wrapped around the legs and
   tied at the waist, resembling baggy trousers
dupatta – long shawl-like scarf draped across the head
   and shoulders
Eid al-Fitr– religious holiday marking the end of
   Ramadan
Eid al-Adha – religious holiday honouring Ibrahim's
   readiness to sacrifice his son
faraa'idh – acts of obligation
gunah – fault, crime, sin, guilt
gunahgar – sinner
hadith – records of events in the life of the Prophet
   Mohammed
halal – permissible under Islamic law

halawa – form of hair removal known as sugaring

haram – forbidden by Islamic law

hijab – meaning 'partition' or 'curtain', colloquially used to refer to a scarf that covers the head

hijabi – person who wears the hijab

imam – mosque leader

inshallah – God willing

ittar – essential oil derived from botanicals

jilbab – long, loose outer garment that covers the entire body

kameez – long tunic

kurta – loose collarless shirt falling either above or below the knee

lehenga – full ankle-length skirt worn at formal or ceremonial occasions

mashallah – God has willed it

masjid – mosque

mullah – Islamic cleric; in Pakistani culture often used in a derogatory way to describe religious leaders who manipulate the masses

madrasa – a school that teaches Islamic theology

Muslimah – Muslim woman

nafs – self, soul, consciousness, ego

nikah – marriage contract

niqab – outer garment covering the head and face, but not the eyes

qadi – judge who administers Islamic law

Quran – the central religious text of Islam

Ramadan – the Islamic holy month of fasting

salwar – loose trousers

salwar kameez – general term for a traditional outfit worn by men and women in various styles, comprising the *salwar* and the *kameez*

Glossary

sharia – Islamic law, derived principally from the
  Quran and the *hadith*

sherwani – men's formal coat-like garment

sunnah – social and legal practice, custom and tradition
  following the example of the Prophet Mohammed

surah – chapter of the *Quran*, each divided into verses

ummah – community (the idea that all Muslims are of
  one body)

zakat – a mandatory charitable contribution; the third
  pillar of Islam

Introduction

In January 2016, the *Daily Telegraph* reported on a private conversation in which David Cameron said he considered Muslim women to be traditionally submissive.[1] The response to his comments was anything but. Photographs of Muslim women holding up placards explaining exactly how they were not #TraditionallySubmissive spread across the internet. These women were everything from 'war survivor' to 'PhD student', from 'mother' to 'doctor'. As I watched it all unfold online, I realized that I was always hearing things 'about' Muslim women. Things 'about' who we were and who we were supposed to be and how we were supposed to act.

When was the last time you heard a Muslim woman speak for herself without a filter? Or outside the white gaze? On her own terms? Or outside the narrative built around us by the media and governments? If Muslim women are to progress in society, if Muslim women are to be treated with respect, then it's so important that we challenge the narrative built around us. It's pretty obvious, isn't it? We should be the authors of our narrative and identity; we should be the ones speaking 'about' us.

It's Not About the Burqa brings together Muslim women's voices. It does not represent the experiences of every Muslim woman or claim to cover every single issue faced by Muslim women. It's not possible to create that book. But this book is a start, a movement: we Muslim women are reclaiming and rewriting our identity. Here are essays about the hijab* and wavering faith, about love and divorce, about queer identity, about sex, about the twin threats of a disapproving community and a racist country, and about how Islam and feminism go hand in hand. Every essay in this book is unfinished, because each one is the beginning of a very necessary conversation.

By using the word 'burqa' on the front cover of this collection of essays, it's frustrating that even now I'm having to engage with a narrative that Muslim women never created. 'Burqa' is a word that has been politicized, and has become synonymous with Muslim female identity: it's just another element in the narrative written around us by others. By engaging with this narrative I hope to dismantle it from within. Muslim women are more than burqas, more than hijabs, and more than society has allowed us to be until now.

We are not asking for permission any more. We are taking up space. We've listened to a lot of people talking about who Muslim women are without actually hearing Muslim women. So now, we are speaking. And now, it's your turn to listen.

Mariam Khan

---

* It's worth pointing out at this stage that though 'hijab' is now more commonly used to describe a scarf that covers the head, in the Quran, the word 'hijab' denotes 'partition' or 'curtain'. 'Hijab' can also refer to a standard of modesty.

1 'David Cameron: More Muslim women should "learn English" to help tackle extremism', *Daily Telegraph* (17 January 2016), https://www.telegraph.co.uk/news/uknews/terrorism-in-the-uk/12104556/David-Cameron-More-Muslim-women-should-learn-English-to-help-tackle-extremism.html

Too Loud, Swears Too Much and Goes Too Far

Mona Eltahawy

A young Muslim woman wrote to me recently to tell me she had reviewed my book, *Headscarves and Hymens: Why the Middle East Needs a Sexual Revolution*, which I published in 2015. In the book, I take a look at women's rights in the Middle East and North Africa in the wake of the 'Arab Spring' revolutions in the region. Like much of my work, it critiques misogyny in my culture and faith background, and calls for social and sexual revolutions alongside the political revolutions of the Arab Spring in order to liberate women from all forms of oppression.

I clicked on the link the young woman sent and read that for a long time she had been scared to read my writing because she had heard that 'Mona Eltahawy is too loud, swears too much and goes too far.'

'Too loud, swears too much and goes too far.'

What a great book title that would make, I thought!

I understood that those descriptors had all been meant as insults. I knew that they were meant as warning signs intended to stop other readers from coming closer. And I knew that for many people they worked. But I took them as compliments.

'Too loud, swears too much and goes too far' sounded just about right. I was proud!

Women are supposed to be 'less than', not 'too much'. Women are meant to be quiet, modest, humble, polite, nice, well behaved, aware of the red lines. They are supposed to tread softly and within their limits.

Patriarchy demands that of all women, but the more women fall within intersections of oppression, the more they are expected to live by those demands, and Muslim women are especially vulnerable to what I call a trifecta of oppressions: misogyny (faced by all women), racism (faced by women of colour) and Islamophobia (faced by Muslims).

Muslim women are caught between a rock – an Islamophobic and racist right wing that is eager to demonize Muslim men, and to that end misuses our words and the ways we resist misogyny within our Muslim communities – and a hard place: our Muslim communities that are eager to defend Muslim men, and to that end try to silence us and shut down the ways we resist misogyny. Both the rock and the hard place are more concerned with each other than they are with Muslim women. They speak over our heads – literally and figuratively. Our bodies – what parts of them are covered or uncovered, for example – are proxy battlefields in their endless arguments. It matters little what we women think because ultimately, both the rock and the hard place agree on and are enabled by patriarchy.

Which is why I am proud to be described as 'too loud, swears too much and goes too far'. When a woman is 'too much', she is essentially uncontrollable and unashamed. That makes her dangerous.

I am especially proud that those attributes are used to describe my writing. One of my literary heroes is queer

Chicana poet, writer and femin
ldúa. In her 1981 essay 'Speaking
to 3rd World Women Writers', An.
importance of writing:

> Writing is dangerous because we are afraid
> writing reveals: the fears, the angers, the stre.
> woman under a triple or quadruple oppression. in
> that very act lies our survival because a woman who
> writes has power. And a woman with power is feared.[1]

I believe the role of the writer is to tell society what it pretends it does not know. The racist, right-wing Islamophobes conveniently ignore – pretend not to know – that misogyny is not exclusive to Muslim men. The Muslim communities that accuse Muslim women who expose misogyny of 'making us look bad' pretend not to know that Muslim men who abuse or assault Muslim women do a sterling job of 'making us look bad' all on their own.

As a feminist, a Muslim and a woman of colour, I am inspired and strengthened by Black American author and civil rights activist Toni Cade Bambara, who told an interviewer in 1982: 'As a cultural worker who belongs to an oppressed people, my job is to make revolution irresistible.'[2]

I have thought long and hard about what an irresistible revolution looks like. For something to be irresistible, I believe it must be a combination of exciting and dangerous – it must entice and frighten. I first came across the word 'feminism' on the bookshelves of my university library in Jeddah, Saudi Arabia. My Egyptian family had moved to Saudi Arabia when I was fifteen years old, after almost eight years of living in first London and then Glasgow. Life for fifteen-year-old girls, between girlhood and womanhood, is hard enough anywhere in the world. I fell into a deep depression soon after we moved to Jeddah. I might not have heard the word 'feminism' yet, but I knew that the way women and girls were treated in Saudi Arabia was wrong and that this was not the Islam I was taught, nor did it represent the home I was raised in. My Egyptian Muslim parents met in medical school and both got scholarships to study for a PhD in medicine in London. They raised my brother and me as the equals we were and with the lesson that education and knowledge were the most important things in life.

When I was nineteen, I finally found, among the books and journals in the library of the university I attended in Jeddah, the word – feminism – that would give me a way to fight back. Feminism saved my mind. There was no women's or gender studies department at the university, so I imagined a renegade librarian or professor had put those books and journals there. Those feminist books were written by women of my cultural and faith backgrounds; women like the Egyptian feminist author and medical doctor Nawal El Saadawi and the Moroccan feminist sociologist Fatema Mernissi, as well as feminists from other parts of the world.

Those books were irresistible. And they terrified me. So much so that I would pick them up, read a few pages, put them down in fear and walk away, only to be drawn back again the next day. I was terrified because I knew on a visceral level that those books – that feminism – would unravel something that I needed, something that would change me forever.

Those books and that feminism were the start of my revolution.

What does such a revolution look like?

A revolution is 'too loud': it defies, disobeys and disrupts patriarchy.

The revolution 'swears too much': it tells racists and Islamophobes to fuck off and that you will never ally with them, and it tells misogynists – our men and other men – to fuck off and that you will not shut up.

Revolutions 'go too far': if your community is ready for you, then you are too late. You must challenge your community. You must throw down the gauntlet of freedom to your community and dare it to accept. Revolutions are by nature uncomfortable. They are meant to discombobulate. How else would the status quo be overthrown? Revolutions rattle the privileged and discomfort the complacent. They are never about the comfortable majority. Rather, it is always the minority, especially those who are caught by the intersection of multiple oppressions, who instigate and inspire.

Who decides who is 'too loud, swears too much and goes too far'? It is usually the 'community'. While that word and concept can provide a sense of solidarity and strength in the face of racism, Islamophobia and other bigotries, it is imperative to ask who speaks for the 'community' and whose interests that community serves.

Too often, 'community' is synonymous with men, and too often those self-appointed male leaders are the ones who determine what is 'too far'. In fact, the word and concept 'community' is much like the word and concept 'culture': for example, a popular way to rein in people – read 'women' – is to tell them that they must not oppose a behaviour or way of being because it is part of the 'culture' or what the 'community' wants. Who determined that it was culture and who speaks for the community? Men and men. That is the simple answer. The more complicated answer is men and men and a system – patriarchy – that enables and protects them at the same time as it socializes women to internalize the dictates of patriarchy and to accept them as culture and as community. If women created culture and community, we would not be accused of 'going too far'.

To be a Muslim woman in the so-called West, where Muslims live as a minority, often beleaguered and subjected to the violence of racism and bigotry, is to stand in the middle point of a see-saw, engaged in a perilous balancing act of telling the rock of racist Islamophobes and the hard place of the community to fuck off, all the while trying not to fall off. I believe in the power of profanity and so I demand that we tell the powers that sit on either side of that see-saw to fuck off. Profanity – especially delivered by women – is a powerful way to transgress the red lines of politeness and niceness that the patriarchy – shared by the rock and the hard place – demands of us as women. I say fuck because I am not supposed to. I say fuck because I believe that the crimes of racism, bigotry and misogyny – enabled and protected by patriarchy – are more profane than swear words. I say fuck because there is nothing civil about racists, Islamophobes and misogynists arguing over my body as if I did not exist.

The revolution is to jump off the see-saw as a first act of transgression on the path to being 'too loud', swearing 'too much' and going 'too far'. It is exhausting, it can be lonely and it will surely gain you the ire of all sides, but it is imperative to make that jump. Refuse to play with either side of that see-saw. In my work, I make it clear that I will never ally myself with the racist Islamophobes against my community, and I let my community know that I will never shut up about its misogyny. I have been accused of giving ammunition to the racist Islamophobes by calling out the misogyny of men of my community, but those misogynist men of my community are never accused of providing plenty of fodder for those racist Islamophobes to use against us. And I skewer the misogyny, as well as the racism and Islamophobia of the right wing. They will never be my friends and I will forever be the enemy of patriarchy, whichever language it speaks or god it worships.

We must jump off that see-saw because neither of its sides cares about us. We must jump into a space we have created, and from which we can launch a revolution against misogyny, racism, Islamophobia and all forms of bigotry. We must create that space for ourselves. So important is the black bisexual poet and activist June Jordan to me that I have tattooed one of her verses onto my arm: We are the ones we have been waiting for.

We are the revolution. Be too loud. Swear too much. Go too far.

---

1   In Cherríe Moraga and Gloria E. Anzaldúa (eds), *This Bridge Called My Back: Writings by Radical Women of Color* (London, 1981)

2   Thabiti Lewis (ed), 'An Interview with Toni Cade Bambara. Kay Bonetti' in *Conversations with Toni Cade Bambara* (Jackson, Mississippi, 2012)

Immodesty is the Best Policy

Coco Khan

I

When I arrive at the community centre, there are already people clad in loose-fitting pastel colours stretching their limbs, shaking out the tension. The occasional 'om' punctures the gentle hum of the overhead fan. I recognize most of the faces – unsurprising, given that this yoga class is part of my job's new wellness programme, and the people I work with are very 'yoga' (they self-define as 'eco', and have names like Orlando and Bruschetta).

The yoga teacher, a pint-size French lady named Aubrey, approaches me. She has a sleeve tattoo and meticulously pedicured toes. I look at them enviously, thinking of my own unloved feet which receive no attention apart from the odd complaint from my boyfriend, yowling in the night when I unwittingly claw him in bed ('it's like sleeping with a snoring falcon,' he'll say). Aubrey even has a toe ring. Show-off.

'What is that?' Aubrey says, pointing to the orange roll of foam I'm holding.

'It's a mat. We were meant to bring our own, right?'

'Why does it have "Blacks" written on it?'

'Oh erm, it's a camping mat.' She stares at me with an

expression I read as disdain but could be pity. 'It's just temporary, my new one is on order.'

Aubrey returns to her spot at the front of the class and I find a space next to June from accounts. 'I just, I didn't want to buy a new one,' I explain to her, 'until I knew yoga was for me. They're not cheap.'

Of course, I do know yoga is for me; it has to be. I need this. Life feels static and exercise brings growth; they say it makes you a better person. Yoga especially. *Health and wellbeing*, I repeat to myself, my little mantra. It has a nice rhythm to it. *Health and wellbeing*. I might not have done much in the way of physical fitness but this feels right. I *am* Indian. Yoga runs through my blood, it's as natural to me as my vitamin D deficiency.

OK, so maybe not *Indian*, Indian; I'm Pakistani, but still, we're similar – same blood, same food, same traditions, hundreds of years living side by side in Punjab. Seventy years of partition couldn't have erased that, right? Yoga is for me, I'm sure of it.

I've not dressed properly and am still pulling off my socks when the class begins – *inhale, one-two-three-four, exhale, one-two-three-four* – and I hurry to unfurl my mat, taking the short end of it where I stand, and letting the rest fall to the floor.

'Fuck,' I say on reflex, louder than I'd like. The last time I used this mat was at a music festival, the debris of which has now been released from the roll, scattering across the floor: scrunched-up Rizla papers, loose tobacco, the odd twig.

Please, no baggies, please, I pray internally as I lay my mat on top of the debris and hope no one saw. Was that June giving me the side-eye? *Inhale, one-two-three-four, exhale, one-two-three-four.*

Into the sequence Aubrey launches, muttering the

odd Sanskrit word, but mostly just speaking to fill the silence. She goes too fast. Just when I think I've understood what I'm meant to do, craning my neck to see if I'm right (and of course I'm not, not even near – how can anyone's foot get there?) she's moved on to the next position. I can feel the stress rising in my body.

Aubrey comes over every so often, to pull my hips back, or to bring me a prop, which I take sheepishly. I look around at my peers, heaving in unison and barely trembling. *Even Fat Frank from sales looks like a swan.*

I push on for as long as I can – *head down, leg up, hold* – but after the third fall I give up and lie flat on my back. Aubrey appears, leaning over me, her soft hair falling from her headband.

'I'm going now anyway,' I say, before she can speak.

II

Funny. Growing up I don't remember anyone talking much about health. Not to me at least. Maybe it did happen. But memories are one of those things. You think all your memories are yours alone, but often they are given by others: versions of events repeated by family, scenes stolen from a movie watched half-sleeping, dreams willed into existence. I want to say that everything that follows here are my memories but I'm not sure. I'm not sure whose they are, or if they indeed ever belonged to anyone. In the end I'm not sure it matters. Sometimes all we know of families are the myths we are told and the fragile heaviness we carry inside, the sound of snapping in the ear.

But I remember the aunties. They liked to gather around and compare notes on minor ailments as a leisurely pastime; an opportunity to flaunt their martyrdom and indulge in a touch of the Bollywood melodrama they enjoyed so much. The sweet spot was having a condition that was in no way chronic or serious (that would be a mood killer) but still involved substantial effort to power through. And the more unnecessary that effort was, the better.

For example, when Auntie Zakiya sprained her ankle after tumbling off her high heels, you still found her the next day hobbling around the desi shops, ankle wrapped above her *salwar* for maximum visibility, telling anyone who'd listen how she simply *had* to come out and get the materials for her daughter's wedding as planned (even though the wedding wasn't for months and the shopping could definitely be done another day). Auntie Zakiya dined out on that sprain for months. 'What a woman!' people would say, 'such a devoted mother,' while other wives smiled through gritted teeth, hoping that the next fall Auntie Zakiya had wouldn't be quite so harmless.

But to us girls, no one talked about health. Rather they talked to us about bodies, flesh. How much of it was on show, where it was shown, to whom it was shown. They talked about the colour of it, the volume of it, the texture of it, and how it looked in photos to be passed around potential suitors.

These days, I don't give a shit about how my body looks, only how it functions. I inherited this apathy towards beauty from my mother. Although, unlike me – with a Body Mass Index which rises with inflation, and a down of dark hair covering every single inch of skin – my mum didn't have to try to be beautiful. She was blessed with measurements to match Marilyn's, and with her face of perfect symmetry turned heads in whichever room she was in.

It was strange to witness the power she had over men, or at least what I thought was power. Single parenthood isn't renowned for its childcare options and so, by default, I was constantly at her side. Inseparable. I was there for every errand, every tedious wait at the pharmacy, every sly put-down from the assessor at the benefits office, every redundancy threat from her supervisor ('your kid being in hospital ain't my problem, love, either come in right now, or don't bother coming back').

And everywhere, there'd be a man, a man with a glint in his eyes.

Mum had won the body lottery. She was a princess whose beauty was worthy of folklore. Radiant Rabia, they called her. I prayed for a fraction of her charm. But for her it was a curse that followed her around, making her skin crawl, filling her veins with fear and paranoia.

She could never enjoy the attention. She was always wondering why they looked. Was it because they knew about the bad thing, the terrible thing she had done?

It wasn't her arranged marriage that was the problem, though that was far from perfect. Her husband had won her hand with tall tales of England and his status in it. She arrived in England a well-educated woman from an influential family, already holding a diploma from the finest art school in Pakistan but with dreams of further education, sophisticated conversation, and all the latest white goods in the kitchen.

Instead she found herself in cramped social housing in a mostly Asian suburb of East London, her dreams of the world shrunk to the four walls she lived between, with only two new infants for company.

Her husband's first wife had been English, and the English wife taught him all the important English things: how to flambé a Christmas pudding; what defines a good Scotch; and the importance of keeping up appearances when inside you are broken.

But while his first marriage didn't last, his fantasy of the elite did. He'd demand that my mother wear makeup, put rollers in her hair, and only wear a mid-length skirt, never trousers. If he was with his friends he'd call her into the room and ask her questions about art before sending her off to make chai. He wanted his peers to envy him for his wonderful, modern wife. But should one of them show it, he'd fly into a jealous rage, banning her from anything but a *salwar kameez*, and telling her whose name was on the lease. He liked to remind her that she was dependent on him in every way.

And then one day, she had had enough. She decided to leave.

But like I said, it wasn't the marriage that was the problem. Nor the divorce. Controversial as it was in the eighties, divorce is halal and even her family back home were surprised she'd put up with him for so long.

My mother adapted to divorced life quickly. She found new friends, mainly other single mums (Kerry, Chantelle, Khadija), as her old ones – the Pakistani Stepford wives – began to distance themselves. They were suspicious of her. After all, could they trust a *divorced* woman in a room with their husbands? And she did notice a shift in how the husbands treated her; how they moved a little closer, how they looked at her with leering, entitled, hungry eyes. She was glad to put all that behind her.

And then there was the new man, the secret new man, Irfan, who was kind, ambitious and funny. She loved him so deeply he would still appear in her dreams decades later. Irfan. She thought Irfan was just like her, a lost soul stuck in an arranged marriage that hadn't played out as he'd hoped. He said he loved her, and was going to leave his wife.

But when the bad thing, the terrible thing happened, the walls started to close in. She'd fallen pregnant with a daughter: me. Irfan needed to make a choice and he did. He chose his wife. Friends, even some family, told Mum to get rid of the baby, using words like 'disgrace' and 'shame'. She refused.

Now it was impossible to escape the feeling of being watched, gossiped about, hated, as a pastime for bored housewives drinking tea.

'Did you know she paints . . . nudes?!' they'd mutter when Mum would emerge from the evening life-drawing class at the college. 'Dirty,' they'd say in hushed tones as she walked past.

'Well, she is a whore, and I am a married man!' Irfan would tell our neighbours when they asked if it was true, about him and her, and the newborn. 'The child isn't mine. Who are you going to believe?' he'd say. 'Me, or her? She is hardly respectable.'

Mum tried her best not to let the black mark placed upon our family suffocate me, and for the most part she was successful. I just assumed the Asian families disliked us for the same reasons the white ones did: we were poor.

As far as I knew she was a 'typical' Pakistani mum. She was suitably disapproving of my own 'improper' behaviour – the drinking, the boys, my total disregard for sound economic choices, and how I'd recoil at the thought of children – but never gave me enough grief for it to make a meaningful difference to my behaviour. Perhaps she had a quiet sympathy. Perhaps she had more important things to think about. Or perhaps I simply remember it wrong.

Even so, I learned a very important lesson. Respectability is an exclusive club, and once you're out, you're out.

III

Today (#snowflake), I am talking at a pace just shy of ranting about modesty culture to Mum, who has said she regrets not doing more exercise when she was younger. 'I'm paying the price for it now,' she says, rubbing her bad knee.

I say I feel the same, that I too wish I'd done more sport at school, and I tell her about the yoga class. I describe my view from the floor, sprawled out and gasping for breath while Fat Frank – who isn't even fat, and presumably earned the name from the Napa '98 holiday he's always shouting about – peacefully holds tree pose in a clinging T-shirt whose slogan reads 'Blink if you want me'. He is so daft I genuinely wonder how he is alive. Mum grimaces.

'I should have encouraged you,' she says. 'I just didn't think of sport as an option for you.'

'That's toxic modesty!' I proclaim, in a voice far too loud for indoors, and with a rhythm too close to 'That's Amore'. 'It prevents women playing sport, from being CEOs . . .'

As if on cue, Mum's eyes begin to glaze over. We've been through this before. She knows what's coming: wokeness. Pure, unfiltered, Twitter-fuelled wokeness.

'Look, I know it's not just a Muslim thing,' I continue to an audience of now zero. 'The notion of modesty is abused by men across the planet – they just give it different names. It winds me up. Why is it always men leading the debate on what's appropriate or not?'

I can feel the desire to evangelize brewing. I try to fight off the temptation but it's futile. Nothing feels as good as testifying.

'Modesty is an instrument of patriarchy, designed to limit women's agency and keep them in line,' I say, beaming.

Mum is now checking her phone, rummaging in her bag and then just looking at her own hand – all things seemingly more interesting than me. I press on.

'Sport is a perfect example. Women are either fully prevented or discouraged from playing because it's immodest. It's either too manly and ungainly, or too tempting for the men. Too tempting, everything is too bloody tempting, what happened to self-control? Like it's our fault they're creeps! Heaven forbid a woman should have a life outside the house and start getting crazy ideas about independence. Why do you think they didn't let women drive in Saudi? It's all connected, Ma!'

'I agree with you,' she interrupts, promptly pulling me off my soapbox. 'But in your case, and me not encouraging you, I didn't care about your modesty. I just never thought about it.'

'But maybe you didn't think of it as an option because toxic modesty narrowed your lens about what life could look like for me,' I reply in a smart-arse tone, and then am immediately repulsed by myself. *Man, I'm such a dick*, I think. *I really must get off Twitter.*

Still, I'm pleased that she was listening. I knew she would be, this is just our merry little dance. We are two halves, yin and yang.

'You know, modesty isn't a dirty word,' she counters. 'People may abuse it, but to be modest is a good thing. Or do you want everyone to be in porn?'

'I don't think the logical next step after questioning modesty is porn, Mum. And anyway, you think everything is porn. You think *EastEnders* is porn.'

I have to be careful here because if she thinks I'm being flippant or disrespectful then this little dance party of ours will descend into a full-on brawl. I call it 'the Westerner Freestyle'. That little flourish is Mum's (solo) pièce de résistance, where she argues that everything I am saying, no matter what it is, is because I am a selfish westerner who knows nothing about anything and she is the wise, selfless easterner, put upon by us kids. It normally ends with her stomping off shouting something about how we'll all regret it when she's dead, although this usually only happens when she's already annoyed about something like me not putting the bins out, which I've done today. (Still, who am I to withhold her moment of melodrama? It is her God-given right.)

'Mum, I know the Quran outlines modesty for all people – men have a hijab too – but you can't deny that the modesty of a woman is all anyone obsesses about. Look what happened to Afia.'

But first, some context.

Afia is one of the daughters of my Auntie Bushra, who I call Auntie B. Auntie B is not my genetic auntie but she may as well be my mum's sister, if not just for the duration of their acquaintance. Bushra is one of the Asian wives from the neighbourhood, the only one who stood by Mum when I was born.

As a child I'd play with Auntie B's kids, whom I loved but whose tall tales could frighten me. The kids were often telling stories of demons and jinn haunting their home, including one who could be summoned by saying its name five times in the mirror (I'd later discover that was actually the plot of the seminal nineties horror movie *Candyman*).

I know kids will be kids. They'll say silly things and use words they don't understand. But I always wondered how much of it they got from Auntie B.

The actions Auntie B undertook because of say, a jinni, were quite spectacular, not to mention the sheer volume of things she defined as *haram*. She could tour her own home and find fifty haram things. *Spices not sealed in airtight containers? Haram! T-shirt with Bart Simpson on a dolphin? The work of Shaitan!*

Mum and she were an unlikely pair. You would think Auntie B would be revolted by my mum but she wasn't. If anything, I think she admired her. She would tell her friends who scowled at us, almost boastfully: 'Oh, Rabia is very modern *yaar*, very cool.'

That's not to say she didn't chastise Mum about being single, or being the only woman in the company she worked for (and therefore having to be alone with men), or countless other things my mum would just roll her eyes at, responding playfully with something like 'you really should get out more' or 'you know, I have a great English phrase I want to teach you, it's called "old wives' tale"'.

And of course when Auntie B had a chance, she'd be working to straighten me out too. Once, she woke me from a post-*SpongeBob SquarePants* nap. 'Wake up, put this on,' she said, holding a headscarf out to me. 'We're going to mosque.'

I panicked at the piece of cloth held out before me; I'd never worn one before. Afia must have spotted my expression because she volunteered to fix it on my head.

At the mosque, we kids were sent off to a separate area. We had Arabic lessons I couldn't follow, and then it was time to pray.

'You've prayed before?' the teacher asked me.

'Yes,' I replied. Which was true, sort of. I'd done it before, one to one in my room, cupping my hands, saying 'bismillah' and letting my heart do the speaking. But I hadn't done this. I still remember it, beat by beat. Every second.

I imitate Afia as closely as I can while she performs her preparations, but before I know it she is at her prayer mat at the back, while I've been moved to a spare place at the front.

Now the teacher is starting – *Allahu Akbar* – and I see that everyone has raised their hands. I copy, but then suddenly everyone's moved into a new position, and again, and again. I'm a few seconds behind everyone no matter what I do, and can feel my heart starting to race. A cold sweat gathers on my brow; the panic is beginning to set in.

I feel eyes burning a hole through me, but when I scan the room looking for . . . what? Posters that explain the next position? An emergency exit? . . . I don't find any eyes except for Afia's, which glare at me in an expression I read as disdain but could be pity.

In the car on the way home from Auntie B's I told my mum about it: that I had tried my best, so why did I feel so ashamed? And then I cried. She pulled the car over in a layby and, grabbing me by the shoulders, said:

'Never, *ever* let people make you feel ashamed for who you are. You know what is right and wrong in your heart, and it is your heart that Allah sees, that I see, and that you have to see every day when you look in the mirror. No one has the right to judge you.'

In between sobs I told her that Auntie B said we were *gunahgar* for not going to mosque.

'Your auntie cannot read. Did you know that? She is illiterate. She has not read the Quran because she cannot. Everything she knows about it is what she's been told.'

'Have you read the Quran?' I asked her.

'Of course!'

'So why don't you go to mosque?'

I saw something unfamiliar flash across Mum's face. Was it shock, or rage? I'd said something she'd heard in the mouths of others before, others who spat and cursed and condemned her. She replied with angry speed:

'In Pakistan I never went to mosque because women never went to mosque and now I'm here and I'm exactly the same but you want to attack me, you want to ask me why I'm not going to the mosque, you want to . . .'

Her voice broke off in a tremble and she turned away from me, staring out of the driver's side window. It was silent apart from the sound of the cars soaring past. I could tell I had hurt her.

'You don't see me criticizing her,' she finally said. 'I could criticize her about her lack of charity – the amount of gold she wears! – or how much her husband smokes and drinks and shouts at her, but I wouldn't.

'Anyway,' she sighed, finally turning the ignition on. 'You shouldn't cry over things she says. Last week she told me the house is cursed. Do you know why? Because her Henry the Hoover went missing. For two hours. It was under the stairs the whole time.'

Afia was the most incredible dancer. She would watch all the Bollywood films and study the dance scenes closely, then she'd lock herself in her room for what seemed like days, and all you'd know of her being alive would be the sound of the cassette player blaring out.

She would dance at Auntie B's parties. Sometimes, if she was dancing to a duet, she would do both parts, jumping between characters. We'd sit against the walls in the room, clapping as she spun around in the centre; elegant long limbs sometimes leaping, sometimes perfectly still.

Afia won every children's Bollywood dance competition by a country mile. She could have easily gone pro. And apparently she was spotted by someone, once. At least that's what I heard. By that time, I'd hit my awkward teenage years, which I chose to spend in skate parks discovering cheap cider and first kisses. Afia had hit puberty too. Her chest had begun to fill out her *kameez*. And that put an end to her dancing dreams.

She got married – it was a love marriage, she chose him – but was divorced a few years later.

Back to the conversation with Mum.

'Imagine if Afia had pursued her dancing dream,' I posit. 'Imagine if she was allowed to be seen, to take up space, and exist in her full capacity. Imagine if all women could do that? Maybe she'd never have chosen the selfish prick she ended up with.'

'Ah yes, you've solved it! You've solved it all!' Mum taunts me. 'Because independent women never end up with rubbish men, do they? It could just be one of those things that happen sometimes. Tell me, what has Afia's teenage hobby got to do with her adult marriage that she chose for herself?'

'Are you joking? Mum, she stopped dancing because she was told women aren't to parade themselves in front of men. And the thing is, it's all fine when it involves boobs and bodies, but they use that same line of thinking for every damn thing. They push you to behave a certain way, which they say is the right way, but why is the right way always less than a man? That's all I'm saying. Less intelligent, less vocal, even less religious – it was you who told me women weren't allowed in the mosque. They keep you in line using religion and then make it hard for you to find out for yourself what the religion is even saying.'

'It's always men versus women with you – if only life was that simple. You know it was Afia's mum who didn't want her to dance. Her dad and brothers said hardly anything.'

'So? That doesn't make it OK. Anyway, women can be instruments of patriarchy too—'

'You and your big words. Here's a word for you: responsibility.'

'—They can push sexist values too, they monitor, they police. Maybe they have to, to survive. Maybe they believe it themselves. I don't know.'

'No, you don't. You really don't.'

IV

A few months after that conversation I get a text from Mum. 'Buy new sari. Afia getting married next week.' *What? Already? How?*

Afia had met someone on one of the online matrimonial (*rishta*) sites, which until that moment I didn't even know existed. I am curious about what happens on these platforms, imagining an ocean of aunties writing slightly insulting profiles of their daughters and nieces. I can see Auntie B's listing for me: 'Looking for man to bring wayward niece back to the light. She cannot cook, likes to argue and could be slimmer. Send help.'

This curiosity is shared by my bezzie mate and serial internet dater, Fizzy (Hafiza), and so in the name of laughter and/or drooling over men, Fizzy sets up a profile. Our expectations are low. The set-up of the site is very traditional: there is no option to list 'not religious' in the mandatory 'religion' field, and certainly no one is cracking any jokes in the 'description' section.

'I bet this site was designed by a man,' I muse.

'Meh, this site is no different from any others,' Fizzy says. 'At least here they're upfront. They're honest about feeling weird about me running a successful business, rather than pretending not to be threatened. And they're definitely honest about looks.'

Fizzy tells me that on OkCupid, a dude might say something like, 'I take care of myself and am looking for a woman who does the same,' meaning, 'I love unrealistic body standards on women.' Here, they are pulling no punches. Maybe it's because for some of them English is a second language, but there truly is no hidden subtext to, 'I don't want fat wife.'

Dissecting the *rishta* sites quickly becomes me and Fiz's favourite pastime.

'Look at this one, Fiz, look at this one. "I am looking for simple, obedient girl." Vom!'

'Why doesn't he just advertise for a chief chapati maker and be done with it.'

'I know, right! This guy says "only virgin!", "no party girls!" He also loves exclamation marks.'

'Translation: I can't be with a woman who has met other men because then she'll know how rubbish I am.'

'And this guy: "I am looking for a ca ... carrier

woman"? I think he means "career", which is lovely, although he can't spell it.'

'Carrier!' she replies, laughing. 'What, like HPV?'

I only catch glimpses of Afia at the wedding, her red *lehenga* and elegant frame, her kohl-painted eyes and glowing skin hypnotizing all the well-wishers crowding around her.

That is until the lights dim suddenly. The speakers are filling the hall with one of those new Bollywood tunes that has a nineties rave flair. A spotlight appears in the centre of the room and there she is, gazelle-like Afia, standing perfectly still, only a pointed toe sticking out from under her *lehenga* skirt. She's wearing a gold jangly ankle bracelet.

She bends her knee and extends it sharply so the bracelet shakes in time to the music. Now her hips are going and applause breaks out like wildfire.

Off she goes, twirling and twirling, when suddenly she is joined in the spotlight by a man, a tall, muscular man with almond eyes and a closely shaved beard, wearing a gold embroidered *sherwani*. It's a duet. They move in unison, mouthing the vocals of their respective parts, miming to each other the song pumping through the speakers.

'Who is that?!' exclaims Fizzy. 'That guy is buffffffff.'

I look at the programme printed on A4 that was handed to me as I entered the wedding. There's a pixelated picture in black and white on the front. I can make out Afia, and there's a blurry man next to her. The man has a beard.

'No way!' I yelp in Fizzy's direction as the penny drops. 'That's Hussein, that's her husband from the *rishta* site!'

'Remind me to look at the site when I get home,' Fizzy says, without returning my gaze. Her eyes are locked on the magnificent couple dancing, synchronized, iridescent.

After the performance I manage to catch Afia.

'You're still an amazing dancer,' I say, gushing. 'I'd love to see you dance again – will you keep up with it?'

'Of course! You can see me dance every week soon. Hussein is helping me, we're going to start a business. A class! I am going to teach ladies to dance like in the films.'

'Wow!'

'Do you know, the white ladies go to the community centre next door and pay twelve pounds to do a Bollywood dance session with a woman named Sandra. Twelve pounds!'

'Well, I am sure it will be a huge success.'

'*Inshallah*, it will be, *inshallah*. You must come. You can come – for free of course – and we can catch up after.'

She looks down at the curve of my full stomach poking out from my sari and smiles at me.

'Seriously, come along. You look like you could use some exercise.

The First Feminist

Sufiya Ahmed

It was Confucius who said that you cannot open a book without learning something. A book can make a home for itself in both your heart and mind, and it can provide the direction you need to succeed in life.

I was twelve years old when my father handed me such a gift. It wasn't a thick book, more like a pamphlet, and the quality of the pages left a lot to be desired as it was printed cheaply, probably in India or Pakistan. The cover was simple: a white background with a crescent and star. The words were written in Urdu, historically the language of the Islamic elite in the latter period of the Mughal Empire.

As a Muslim of Indian heritage, in addition to learning to recite the Quran in Arabic, I was expected to learn to speak, read and write Urdu from a young age. The sole purpose of acquiring this language was so that I could learn about Prophet Mohammed (peace be upon him). I read about his life from his birth to his childhood, when he was orphaned after the death of his widowed mother and raised by his paternal grandfather, then later his uncle, in Mecca. I learned about his young adult life when he developed a reputation as an honest and trustworthy trader, all the way to the man he became around the age of forty when he received the revelation about the One God, the Most Merciful and the Most Just.

The book my father gave me, however, was not about Prophet Mohammed, and although flimsy in appearance, it was the one that sowed the seeds of feminism in my mind – it taught me that the foundations of my faith were fairness and justice, and that God does not promote gender inequality.

The book was about a woman who lived fourteen hundred years ago. Her name was Khadija bint Khuwaylid, and she was the beloved wife of Prophet Mohammed. They married when he was twenty-five years old and she was forty, and remained together until her death. Although polygamy was standard practice in their tribe, the Prophet was faithful to her throughout their marriage, refusing to take a second wife.

Khadija is known to Muslims as the Mother of Believers for her position as the Prophet's first wife. She also holds the title of First Muslim as she was the first person to accept the Prophet's message of the One Merciful God. But what fascinated me about Khadija had nothing to do with her role as a wife and mother. It was her professional life and business acumen that drew me to her like a magnet and made her my role model. And in all the times when I have felt othered or my confidence took a knock, she came to the rescue to lift me right back up.

Prophet Mohammed's tribe were known as the Quresh, a community of traders who lived in Mecca. Within that tribe, Khadija was a successful businesswoman. Actually, let's not talk down her achievements. She was *the* wealthiest merchant in Mecca, and was known as Al-Tahira, the Pure One, for her honesty and integrity.

The book my father gave me celebrated Khadija. It celebrated her wealth, and most importantly it celebrated the fact that she was reliant on no man. Her feminism was about a woman's right to be independent of anyone else. Khadija's business and her money belonged to her, and that gave her freedom.

It was this sense of freedom that really struck me. It was the opposite of what my patriarchal Asian culture tried to enforce on women, and what was enacted and enforced by women who were complicit in their own oppression, the dreaded 'auntie-jis'. In the eyes of the auntie-jis in my community, all women belonged to fathers, brothers, husbands and finally, in old age, to adult sons. A woman could not have full autonomy over her life, and all choices were steered towards the benefit of her male relatives.

Even as a young child I was fully aware that I was different from everyone else because my mother had been a single parent who had then remarried. It was a courageous and unique thing for a young immigrant woman to do. And yet I was surrounded by a community that disapproved of this sort of independence. Any attempt to challenge the traditional roles was met with disapproval that quickly spread through gossip and manifested as social control. 'What will people say?' is a line that many Asians use to control the choices of their children, especially daughters. 'Don't stain the family honour' is another line drummed into young minds, as if girls and women are walking vessels through which the family can be judged on worthiness and respect. So there was another very personal reason why Khadija's independence resonated with me. It made me realize that the choice to live on one's own terms was not forbidden in my religion. It gave me the choice to reject a patriarchal culture that controlled women's movements, and especially the ones that boxed them into relationships that were unhappy or violent. And it became all the more important to me because of my own mother's experience.

I was born into a broken home. My mother arrived as a seventeen-year-old in the 1970s to an industrial mill town in Greater Manchester. She made the journey from India to marry a distant relative in a match arranged by her mother, my nannyma. My mother initially lived with her older cousins, sisters who had followed the same path a few years earlier to marry men chosen by their parents.

She has often spoken of the shock she and her cousins felt at the life they were expected to lead. These young women hailed from middle-class landowning families in Gujarat, west India. They grew up with wealth and status, and were now expected to live in tiny terraced houses, cold and damp with outside loos.

Within weeks of my mother's arrival to this new land, she dutifully married my biological father. The marriage failed to last six months and they separated. Concerned for her daughter thousands of miles away, my nannyma paid for my mum to fly back home to India.

It was only after she returned to India that my mother revealed to my nannyma that she was pregnant. In many other families this news would have been met with consternation. Traditional roles dictate that daughters should remain within their marriages, regardless of their treatment. My nannyma did not subscribe to this view. She was a strong woman of independent mind, a financial supporter of poor widows and divorcees in the village.

She believed in a woman's right to not just live on her own terms, but to live those choices with dignity and respect. Naturally, she fully supported her own daughter and celebrated my birth. As the first grandchild I was absolutely adored by my grandparents and uncles and aunts. And it did not matter that I was a girl rather than a boy. Stories of boys being valued over girls is nothing new in South Asia. Boys are regarded as breadwinners for elderly parents, whereas girls are seen as burdens that have to be married off with dowries. I have engaged in enough women's rights activism to know that the belief 'sons are better than daughters' is a huge problem in some parts of the world, especially in India.

For those who have little knowledge of Islam, there is the assumption that Muslim women's oppression stems from Islamic teachings. This is simply not the case. In fact Muslim imams preach about the value of daughters, often citing that 'a daughter opens the gates of paradise for a father'. Indeed, the person most beloved to Prophet Mohammed (pbuh) was his youngest daughter, Fatima.

Islamic teachings are clear that a father has to fulfil his duty to raise and care for his daughters, and that the obligations go beyond providing financial support. He must provide a safe, peaceful and loving home environment that is conducive to his daughter's overall spiritual and moral development.

My mother's family has always believed that their faith teaches them to value daughters, but not everyone in the wider community agreed. The imams' sermons about valuing daughters fell on many deaf ears, allowing the cultural practice of viewing daughters as burdens to flourish. The labels of 'single parent divorcee' and 'fatherless girl' were attached to my mother and me as news of my birth spread.

My mother faced a stark choice.

On the one hand, we could remain at her parents' home, under their protection.

Or she could return to England with me as a baby of British descent. My mother knew that England could give me everything that would be denied to me in a wealthy but parochial rural community that dictated that girls remain in the home. England could give me an education, and allow me to stand on my own two feet. It could give me what she craved. Independence.

My mother chose England.

And she chose it for me.

She was nineteen years old when she found the courage to leave the security of her parents' home once again, and return to England so that she could give me a different life. Clutching her one-year-old baby in her arms, she waved goodbye to my devastated nannyma and boarded the plane on the Bombay tarmac for Heathrow.

Now back in England, my mother did not return to the town where she married. She made a clean break and settled in Bolton to be close to her cousins, who offered friendship and support. As a curious teen, I once asked her about our early life together in the UK, and she reluctantly revealed the hardship she faced as a single parent divorcee in the 1970s. She spoke of the poverty; the small rooms she rented; the rats scurrying in the corners; the damp in the walls and the freezing cold of northern England winters. It broke my heart to learn that she had endured all this so that I could have the opportunities of a British girl.

When I was six years old she visited another cousin in London and fell in love with the big city and its warmer temperatures. She refused to return to the north after that. A year later, my nannyma arranged her second marriage. It was to the man whom I consider to be my father, the one who gave me the book about Khadija.

A feature of all migration is the transference of culture from the old to the new land. My mother may very well have left the rural Indian village behind, but the label of 'fatherless child' did not delay in following us to our new home. That parochial mindset was in full evidence in the British Asian community of the 1970s and 1980s.

It was First Lady of the United States of America Eleanor Roosevelt who said that 'no one can make you feel inferior without your consent'. Although I believe this with a passion now, as a child I completely absorbed the feelings of inferiority that adults put upon me as the child of a first, unsuccessful marriage. Looking back now, perhaps it was pity rather than disapproval that was being directed at me. Whatever it was, it was a form of otherness and it distressed me. I dreaded weddings and other large community gatherings because I knew there would be interest in me as a conversation point. This left a mark on my self-confidence, and was one of the reasons why I gravitated towards the anonymity and safety of the public and school libraries.

Then I turned twelve and I suddenly had this powerful book about Khadija bint Khuwaylid in my hand, given to me by a man who was not my biological father but who raised me proudly as his own daughter along with my new siblings. Khadija's independence rendered the views of the self-appointed guardians of parochial culture irrelevant. I decided that I would no longer allow the auntie-jis to make me feel as if I were a second-class citizen. Stripping them of their power to affect me was like turning a corner. I was now a teenager who no longer cared, rather than the child who always sought the adults' approval.

I attended a secondary girls' school where I was taught that I could achieve anything I wanted. Without the distraction of boys, or having to give up space to them, I spent my teenage years developing the belief that I absolutely deserved to be successful and that I didn't need to sit on the sidelines as the nearest man took the lead.

Growing up with access to free books from my school and public libraries had raised my aspirations. Through reading, I explored worlds that were different and distant from my tiny bubble of the local high street, my school and the council estate. I knew that one day I would escape the block of flats that was my home and become successful and independent, just like Khadija. Throughout it all was my mother's quiet encouragement. An education and financial independence would mean that I would never have to suffer the poverty that she experienced as a single mother. It would mean that I would never have to be reliant on the goodwill and charity of relatives if I ever found myself alone.

My dream was to become a children's author. Roald Dahl and Enid Blyton provided the inspiration and I was convinced that I could become a published novelist. Although money was tight, my mother made savings from her weekly shopping budget to buy me a typewriter after I had convinced her that I needed one in order for my dream to come true. (It was still the eighties and computers were those odd machines that the older year groups were allowed to use in IT.)

I still remember that Saturday afternoon in Argos when I was allowed to choose my gift. It was a cream-coloured typewriter with black keys, and it was my pride and joy. A year later, when I was fourteen, I sent off my first children's novel to Puffin Books. Unsurprisingly, I didn't hear back, but I was not deterred. One day I would succeed, just like Khadija. It was only a matter of time.

Throughout my early teens, the security of a girls' school and loving, supportive parents protected me from the misogyny that existed in the real world. But when I hit eighteen, everything changed.

It was almost as if I had been teleported back to my childhood, before I had discovered Khadija. The only difference was that now it wasn't the auntie-jis making an issue of my presence, but Muslim men who challenged me for daring to exist outside my traditional Muslim woman box.

It was freshers' week at university and I was sitting with a group of fellow students in the cafeteria. Everyone was being pleasant, assessing each other for possible friendship. Sitting across the table from me was a young man of Pakistani origin. Perfectly nice. Perfectly polite. Perfectly behaved within the bounds of social convention with people that he deemed to be worthy of respect. But what became very clear in the next few minutes was that I, as an Asian Muslim woman, was not deemed to be worthy, and it was this total lack of respect that permitted him to cross the boundaries of social interaction.

He leaned forward and fixed me with a direct stare. 'What are you doing here?'

I gazed back at him, somewhat confused. 'Sorry?'

'I'm asking you directly.' He sprawled his body over the chair, his legs wide apart, deliberately taking up more than his share of the space. 'How come you're allowed to be here?'

I still didn't understand the question. What was he referring to?

'Well, I did History, Law and Sociology. What did you do?'

The look on his face changed. The smugness evaporating to be replaced by pure disdain. It made me feel unnerved, at a loss as to why another person should feel such hostility towards me. He was clearly boosted by the uneasiness evident on my face.

'No, I meant how did your father allow you to attend university? You're a Muslim girl. You should not be here.'

I couldn't believe my ears. Redness slowly crept up my neck to flood my face, but he was enjoying my reaction. Why wouldn't he? He sincerely believed that I had no right to be there. In order to feel superior, he needed to make someone else feel inferior. And I was the sitting duck.

The rage that I had locked away as a child when I had been made to feel othered for being the daughter of a divorcee was unleashed. As a little girl I had lacked the words and the courage to allow me to give a retort so cutting that the abuser would think twice before trying to bully again. I had the words and the courage now.

Raising my voice so that others could hear, I delivered the line. 'I have every right to be here. Your family must be proper backwards to keep daughters locked up at home.'

The cocky expression vanished. My retaliation was the last thing he expected and he didn't know how to react. My insult directed at his own family's shortcomings had rendered him speechless.

I wish I had known at the time that the person credited for founding the oldest existing, first degree-awarding educational institution in the world, the University of Al Quaraouiyine in Fes, Morocco, in the year 859, was a Muslim woman. Alas, I did not know about the founder Fatima Al-Fihri and so, although I walked away from the table with the last word, I would be lying if I didn't admit that the exchange had rattled me. Worst of all, the tiniest doubt of my right to be at university started to take hold in my mind. Did the idiot have a point? He had spoken with such confidence and authority that I questioned my own right to occupy the space that I had worked so hard to reach, with the blessing of my parents. I felt minimized and alienated. As if my being an Asian Muslim woman somehow rendered me a second-class citizen behind all the white English people and the Asian Muslim men. I had been here before with the auntie-jis' disapproval in my early childhood.

Then my role model came to the rescue. I reminded myself of Khadija, the Mother of Believers, and her successful, independent position in Mecca. I knew that if she had existed on her own terms, then no nineteen-year-old misogynist could question my right to exist as I chose.

There is a saying that I have always lived by and I would recommend it to every ambitious woman, regardless of faith and race. When a woman travels from A to B, she will encounter mad dogs along the route who will bark at her. Some men (and there are many women too) will always shout discouragement to a woman on her path to success. The thing to do is to ignore them. Never stop to reason with a mad dog.

Emerging into the big wide world after university, my dream to become a published author was still far away. I dutifully bought the *Writers' & Artists' Yearbook* and sent off three sample chapters and a synopsis to an endless list of agents. Rejection letters piled up as well as my father's mutterings that I shouldn't put all my eggs in one basket. Taking his advice, I started looking for a 'proper' job.

In my twenties I enjoyed a successful career in advertising before giving up the private sector money to work in the Houses of Parliament as a researcher. However, society's patriarchal chains are strong. Despite my role model and the advantage of a girls' school education, there were many days when I felt I didn't belong, and that I didn't deserve the career and success I had. You see, Khadija allowed me to believe that I had the right to be there, but I hadn't yet joined the dots enough to allow me to believe that I alone was responsible for my success. For a very, very long time I believed that I owed it to stumbling along and hitting gold. There were many times when I felt that I had simply been lucky.

I made a terrible habit of undermining my own achievements. Discounting praise became second nature. I think it had something to do with the very British practice of being self-deprecating. The worlds of advertising and Parliament are filled with white upper-middle-class men, many of whom boast Oxbridge on their CVs. They lived privileged childhoods that I only saw in my library books. Being self-deprecating came naturally to many of them and I soon picked up on the habit. You see, in my twenties and thirties, I always felt that to accept praise of any kind was to show myself up to be an awful, boastful person. It was OK for the Americans to do it, but hey, we're British and we don't sing our own praises. Humility was all.

However, I discovered over a gradual period of time that when I was dismissive of praise, my colleagues accepted my denial of achievement at face value. It was almost as if they thought, 'Well, if Sufiya says she doesn't deserve the praise, then she probably doesn't.' But they never accepted it as truth when my white, upper-middle-class colleagues did it. Now aware of this discrepancy, I made the conscious decision to stop undermining myself. The reminder of Khadija's success gave me pride in my own achievements.

Her status as the most successful businessperson in her tribe also helped to counter the moments of self-doubt that crept in when I felt overwhelmed by my surroundings. Despite growing up in London, only eleven miles from Parliament's location, no school trip had ever been arranged to visit the building. Instead, as a teen I had gazed upon the Palace of Westminster from a car window en route to Heathrow airport many times, never believing that I had the right to step inside like every other British child. The Houses of Parliament can be an intimidating environment with its history and power, and I felt that every day I was working there. But the Houses of Parliament is also a place to usher in change. With the memories of my childhood in mind, I set up the BIBI Foundation, a non-profit organization to invite diverse and underprivileged school children to tour the Houses of Parliament – I wanted other kids to see inside and know that they too might one day walk these corridors.

Working within the walls of Parliament also brought me into closer contact with women's rights activism. Different campaigns highlighted different injustices. Some were common to all women, regardless of race and religion, like rape and domestic violence. Others were more specific to different cultures, like forced marriage and female genital mutilation.

It was the disparity between the life of Khadija and the lives of some modern British Muslim women, still repressed under cultural rules in the twenty-first century, that inspired me to become a women's rights activist. It irked me that some non-Muslims viewed Islam as oppressive to women, without any understanding of the patriarchal structures that allow such practices to flourish. It pained me further to realize that there were many Muslim women and men who were simply not aware of the gender equality that exists in the Islamic faith. This was through no fault of their own, as they were simply not taught about the rights of women in Islam. It made me realize then how fortunate I had been to have received the book on Khadija as a twelve-year-old, and that I should make an effort to share my view of my role model as an example of the gender equality that my faith promotes.

It was this activism that inspired me to write *Secrets of the Henna Girl*, a novel about a British Asian girl facing the prospect of a forced marriage. It is a story about hope, courage and empowerment, and one that I needed to write, not just to raise awareness of women's rights in Islam, but also to offer a different perspective to the narrative that dominates bookshop shelf space about Muslim women. These include the books where Muslim women seem to have little to no agency and are waiting for a saviour to rescue them; where there is absolutely zero independence.

I won't deny that my novel begins with the teenage protagonist as a victim, but she stands up to the bullying which is inflicted on her in the name of family honour, and she does this through the strength that she derives from the faith's teachings about the rights of a woman to choose her own spouse, to be free of harm, and to have her choices respected.

I put my heart and soul into writing *Secrets of the Henna Girl* and after completing the umpteenth draft, was delighted that Puffin Books agreed to publish it. After years and years of trying, I finally became a published author in my mid-thirties. It was my first book and it felt right to dedicate it to the memory of my nan-nyma, who had selflessly allowed her daughter and granddaughter to leave the rural village for the opportunities my mother wanted for me in England.

Today, my role model Khadija is never far away when I engage in panels or workshops about *Secrets of the Henna Girl* and gender equality.

I explain how Khadija's existence cemented my belief that my faith could never promote inequality. When I have been faced with the argument that women are not equal to men by Muslims who doubt that gender equality exists in Islam, I have always given this scenario:

Imagine a woman stealing an apple. Now imagine a man stealing an apple.

Theft is forbidden in Islam.

The sin of stealing for both a man and a woman is equal. In no verse in the Quran, or in any *hadith*, is it written that a woman's sin is less than a man's. Islam is very clear that a woman's capability to do wrong is equal to a man's.

How then is she not equal to him in all other matters?

For me Khadija was the first feminist and she inspired me to become one. She taught me to stand up for women's rights, for girls' rights, and to challenge inequality and misogyny, both cultural concepts which are designed to serve the patriarchal society structures that benefit men and reduce women to subservient roles.

Above all, Khadija taught me that I had every right to exist as I chose.

Just like she did as the wealthiest merchant in Mecca.

On the Representation of Muslims*

*Terms & Conditions Apply

Nafisa Bakkar

In recent years attempts to represent Muslims have been made across mainstream culture: TV shows, magazines, media outlets, adverts and brands. And yet, every time a documentary airs on Channel 4 or the BBC, be it *Muslims Like Us* or *Islam, Women and Me*, Muslims take to social media proclaiming that these shows do not represent Muslims or the British Muslim experience. I myself have found it difficult to see representation in these forums, and I know I'm not alone. This is one of the reasons why I started Amaliah.com two years ago with my sister Selina Bakkar; it was our own way of trying to work to improve what the state of representation looked like.

Amaliah is a media platform dedicated to amplifying the voices of Muslim women through articles, videos, podcasts and events led by Muslim women. In the last two years we've built our community of contributors to over 200 Muslim women from around the world, many of whom have never felt comfortable sharing their voice on mainstream platforms. We wanted to be able to encourage a conversation that wasn't always made up of Muslim women talking about the hijab or why they weren't oppressed. Amaliah was created as a space for Muslim women to exist on their own terms, whether that was talking about dodgy dates, mental health, significant cultural moments or smashed avo on sourdough.

Since we launched Amaliah, my own thoughts on identity and what it means to be represented have evolved. Why do we need representation, and if it is a means to an end, what is the end goal? Should we be holding each other to account or should we be treating a Muslim woman the same way we do – say – an influencer that is not from the faith, where we take no issue with her being on magazine covers or in music videos? And if not, what is it that we should take issue with? My thoughts on representation, its merits and pitfalls, will forever be evolving, but this is where they have got to.

To date, much of the conversation around Muslim women has its roots in othering and stereotypes. Remember David Cameron alluding to the fact that Muslim men are radicalized because Muslim women are traditionally submissive?[1] Or headlines positioning Muslim women as stereotype-breakers for the smallest of deeds? Representation of Muslim women flip-flops between fitting a stereotype or breaking one, not the middle ground where most of us are. The use of a Muslim woman is seemingly dependent on what's being promoted or sold. When the Muslim woman is discussed in a political light or in reference to government strategy it seems representation is synonymous with a burqa- or niqab-wearing woman. When it's fashion or beauty, she takes the form of a hijabi influencer.

The othering of Muslims can be explained partly by the concept of the 'default man'. In his book *The Descent of Man*, Grayson Perry writes about the way the world revolves around the idea of the default man, who is white, middle-class, heterosexual and usually middle-aged. The default man is seen as 'the reference point from which all other values and cultures are judged'; he and what he represents is the backdrop against which all other identities exist.[2] Whether it is halal meat or the hijab, any deviation from the blueprint of the norms of the default man poses a threat to the standards society upholds. And I would extend Perry's idea to assume that the default man is also one of secular ideology. If a 'default' existed within Muslim communities as a sub-group, it would probably be a South Asian, middle-aged, cis, Sunni man. His is the face you often see on event posters about Muslims. He is the one who sits on mosque and Muslim charity committee boards. So for Muslim women the default within both the Muslim communities and 'mainstream' communities is something they can never be: male.

There is a monolithic brush that all Muslims are painted with because of our common thread: the belief in Allah, his messengers and his book. We of course often refer to ourselves as one *ummah*, one body, but this shouldn't be taken to mean that we are all the same without variations in practices and ideas. Therefore, in order for Muslim women to thrive in our current climate, we need to start from a point at which the default, if we must have one, is inclusive and mindful of the many intersections that exist, not predicated on white males being the standard. As Muslims we must also question why our default must be predicated on another human being. We've seen many Muslim women align themselves with feminist movements in order to uphold and fight for the rights that have been given to us in Islam, and those women have continuously come under scrutiny, one of the critiques being that these movements are predicated on the equality of the sexes rather than equality in the eyes of our creator, Allah:

> What we so often forget is that God has honored the woman by giving her value in relation to God—not in relation to men. But as Western feminism erases God from the scene, there is no standard left—except men. As a result, the Western feminist is forced to find her value in relation to a man. And in so doing, she has accepted a faulty assumption. She has accepted that man is the standard, and thus a woman can never be a full human being until she becomes just like a man.[3]

If our feminism is not intersectional then we run two risks: that we will never escape this idea of the default being male, and that we dilute our faith in our attempts to mould Islam to make it more palatable to outsiders.

When I first began considering the issue of representation, I didn't go much further than wanting to see myself. In 2015, when we were creating Amaliah and entered the start-up scene, I saw an industry filled with the default man. It was overwhelmingly white men who held the keys to the doors that I needed to get through. Every event, every panel I went to, was made up of white men, and even in 2018 we saw headlines like 'More people called David and Steve lead FTSE 100 companies than women and ethnic minorities'.[4]

Everything I saw reinforced the idea that perhaps this wasn't for me and I constantly sought out people who I could connect with. When I found out that the CEO of PepsiCo was an Indian woman by the name of Indra Nooyi, I became fixated on listening to podcasts and interviews with her. Seeing women like Indra, with whom I shared an Indian heritage, gave me hope. I longed to see company founders that looked like me: I was searching for validation that I could do it if they could. Then, in 2015, I watched Alex Depledge, then founder of Hassle.com and now of Resi.co.uk, on TV, and I immediately thought *I need to talk to her.* This was a woman who was successful in the tech scene, and when I got in touch, she agreed to become one of my first mentors. It was then that I realized the true value of seeing even a small part of myself – in this case, my gender – in someone in a position I aspired to. For me, Alex represented part of who I was, and I could relate to her in a way that helped me feel like I could also carve a path out for myself. Since then I've spoken at a number of events about starting a business because I realize the value of young women hearing from a female, ethnic minority founder – it eases that debilitating crisis of confidence.

At the same time we were embarking on Amaliah in late 2015, H&M launched its recycling campaign, 'Close the Loop'. The campaign video included more than seventy individuals and it was clear that H&M was making a point about diversity, but the world's attention focused on the two seconds featuring Mariah Idrissi, who then went on to be dubbed one of the first global Muslim hijab-wearing models. Idrissi – by her own admission – was overwhelmed by the response which, overall, seemed to be one of praise: H&M and Mariah Idrissi were breaking barriers, they said.

And we saw it again and again. Dolce & Gabbana released their *abaya* range, Amazon had an interfaith Christmas advert, Halima Aden hit the runway, and Mattel produced a hijabi Barbie doll. Nike released a sports hijab, Tesco featured a Muslim family in their Christmas advert, *that* L'Oréal campaign with Amena

Khan went live, and even the army launched a recruitment video showing a Muslim man praying while his comrades waited for him. Representation had arrived! The Muslim moment really was here and it was matched with headline upon headline about the Muslim pound, how much Muslim consumer segments were worth, and how it was Muslim women in particular who were breaking stereotypes. Even Amaliah benefited from the wave; we were overwhelmed with the number of media outlets that wanted to cover our work, from the *Guardian* and the *Metro* to CNN, *Forbes*, *Wired* and the *Telegraph*. If we had launched even a year earlier, I doubt that this would have been the case. But there was a backlash. When campaigns like the Nike sports hijab and the hijabi Barbie came around, for some it felt like independent Muslim business owners were getting elbowed out. Hijabi dolls and sports hijabs already existed, created by Muslims; however, it was only when global brands came up with the same concept that the world applauded.

This sudden rise in the visibility of Muslim women in the mainstream, the sudden presence in fashion campaigns of uber-cool, trendy hijabis, forced me to rethink what representation means and if it was even meaningful in its current form. Yes, advertising and media has a *huge* effect on how we view society and its groups, but why had representation in this capitalist machine suddenly become such a priority? It wasn't the fact that I was now seeing Muslim women everywhere that unsettled me. It was that it seemed as though representation within a secular system with the primary purpose to make money for large companies had been held up as the solution to racism, to othering and to ignorance. But surely, we couldn't ignore the backdrop to all that existed: Trump, Brexit and increasing hate crime towards Muslims.

I wondered if we had been distracted by all of this representation politics. Was it meaningful to anyone but the influencer herself to be on the front cover of a magazine? Part of our work at Amaliah is about collaborating with brands and agencies to have access and offer value to the community we have built. We see our work as a tool for cultural change, but what sort of change we want to be associated with is something we have questioned. I sometimes found myself annoyed when I saw a campaign featuring a Muslim woman, because I have walked into brands, into agencies, and seen virtually zero diversity. It seemed as though 'seeing Muslims' was being over-indexed by those in the mainstream. And an uneasy sentiment began to rise, which we saw communicated by contributors on Amaliah.com time and time again. It seemed the archetype of what an acceptable Muslim woman should look like was being created out of this push for representation. This concern was expressed by Afia Ahmed in an article on Amaliah titled 'How the Turban Hijab Became a Symbol of the Modern Muslim Woman':

> Commercialisation didn't make hijab easier, it changed what it is. People no longer ascribe [sic] to the hijab, they ascribe [sic] to a fashion trend [...] The turban [headscarf] has become the symbol of the New Muslim Woman. A marker of success, liberation, and modernity. Yet this symbol supposedly aiming to help Muslim women feel included, for many, has done the exact opposite of what it set out to do. In including one faction of society, it has ostracized another, and a number of Muslim women no longer feel represented.[5]

For Afia, such representation didn't allow for authenticity, and had only paved the way to making a more palatable version of Muslims. Thinking about how Muslim women were temporarily being cast made me realize that the whole representation process often employs the short-term labour of minorities, and I can't help but compare this representation frenzy to a puppet show in which we are not permitted to construct ourselves on our own terms. Our identity is rented out in perfect models; we are on a short-term lease. We cannot deny that there is a cookie-cutter model of a Muslim woman that is seen in campaigns, movies, the media and amongst brands. The current cookie cutter is light skinned, wears a hijab and is normally a fashion or beauty influencer. This is the West's version of the default Muslim woman and we cannot deny she is an extension of Eurocentric beauty ideals. If we match up to agency briefs, if we fit into the existing set-up, then perhaps we can have equality – but an equality that feels increasingly superficial and lacking in authenticity. Which led me to ask, was I just bitter that we were the ones in front of the camera, rather than behind it? Would it make a difference to how we perceived representation if we were actually the people calling the shots? Was it just that it all felt a little disingenuous to be pushing an aesthetic, when that was being confused with pushing the values of Islam and the opinions and identities of Muslim women?

The Amena Khan L'Oréal haircare campaign was just one of the many moments that told us that brands wanted Muslims as an aesthetic, nothing more and nothing less. Khan was part of a haircare campaign which broke the internet, with the media claiming she had made history and broken barriers as the first hijabi model to star in a global mainstream hair campaign.[6] But Khan stepped down from the campaign within days after tweets of hers from 2014 surfaced, which 'lamented the killing of Palestinians and the illegal occupation of Palestinian land, and praised some world leaders who had spoken out against Israel as it waged a brutal war', according to Al Jazeera.[7] Khan went on to issue an apology for the tweets, but the damage was done, and the message was clear: We want your hijabs but we don't want your thoughts; we only want diversity for the pictures. And furthermore, the backlash convinced those with platforms that they had to audit their accounts, their opinions and their pasts, to ensure that they didn't 'offend', so that they would never have to write an apology after being dropped from a campaign.

What is the point of being represented if it is only our image that is invited to the table? Is a Muslim woman being in a fashion campaign the end in itself? Is the hope that, in making Muslim women more visible, it will open doors for others? As I've thought more about this, I've also found myself questioning the use of the term 'influencer'. While we refer to these people as influencers, due to the financial model through which they tend to make an income – i.e. working with brands – influencers themselves inevitably become influenced. At the moment, many Muslim brands do not have enough spending power (or desire) to engage in influencer marketing. What this means is that larger brands are left with the whole playing field and thereby dictate the terms of influence. Amaliah also makes money by collaborating with brands, but time and again, we have had to turn down work with certain companies due to a clear clash in values. There is no doubt this is all a learning process, and we will not always get it right, but that is part of why I feel we must stop to critique and learn from what has happened. Representation is meant to exert some sort of cultural influence, but that influence can often be skewed depending on who holds the keys to the wider platforms.

The story of Sudanese-Australian Yassmin Abdel-Magied is another interesting case study. Abdel-Magied believed that she could outperform her identity. She thought that if she followed the right social cues, if she behaved like a 'model minority', in a way in which her banter was understood amongst white men, and if she ensured that she contributed to society and her country, she would be celebrated and accepted. But one seven-word Facebook post out of line and her theory failed. On Anzac Day, Australia's national day of remembrance originally introduced to honour the Australian and New Zealand Army Corps (ANZAC) who fought at Gallipoli in the First World War, many use the phrase 'Lest We Forget'. Yassmin wanted to 'make my sentiment more inclusive than just those who fought in that war', and extended her post to others that she felt we should not forget. Her post read, 'LEST. WE. FORGET. (Manus, Nauru, Syria, Palestine . . .)'. She took it down almost immediately (a friend had seen it and thought some may find it offensive) and issued an apology, but within days she was on the cover of national newspapers, and receiving messages saying she should self-deport. She was made an example of: as an immigrant Muslim woman of colour, her opinions were not welcomed. They were not judged as the opinions of any other intelligent, thinking Australian citizen, and she was deemed 'ungrateful'. She found herself becoming the most hated Muslim woman in Australia and eventually felt she had to leave the country. As a member of a minority she had terms and conditions to her free speech.[8]

In the same way, Stormzy, the UK's grime artist sensation, was hailed as British homegrown talent until he decided to criticize the government, at which point he was aptly reminded by the media that he was in fact born to Ghanaian parents who had benefited from this country's generosity. He too should be grateful.[9]

Scandalous opinions aside, seeing all these Muslim women in the limelight and being heralded for breaking barriers makes me question what it means for us collectively. I think of the campaigns, I think of the tokenism, and I question what it actually does for Muslim women beyond a temporary jolt of excitement or acceptance. In *Lean Out* by Dawn Foster, a rebuttal of Sheryl Sandberg's *Lean In*, Foster speaks about the 1 per cent corporate feminism that serves the few.[10] She believes that corporate feminism is convenient for capitalism as 'focusing on individual success stories is far easier than changing the way business operates – but doesn't actually improve women's working lives'.[11] In fact, celebrating individuals also plays a role in cementing the problem – it means we act as if the gates are suddenly wide open or the glass ceiling and structural inequalities no longer exist. We create an illusion that success is at the tip of our fingers.

But seeing the likes of Fatima Manji on Channel 4 reporting the news or Nadiya Hussain with her own cooking show on the BBC should not lure us into the false belief that now everyone can make it because 'they did', and if you can't it is not down to the structure and the process, it is down to individual action. I have often felt like a fraud for speaking at events, because I worry that I may be fuelling the idea that 'you can do it' – you just have to have resilience and drive and you can achieve anything. But just because I find myself running a business as a Muslim woman, it does not mean that every Muslim woman is now afforded the pathway to do so. While I do not doubt that seeing some part of yourself in such roles has an effect on your own perception of self, we must not think this is the be all and end all of ensuring we are afforded equality. As Asim Qureshi argues:

> Representation is sold to our communities as the holy grail of acceptance. If a Muslim becomes a Member of Parliament, he has not only achieved the highest status of representation, but also then becomes an exemplar for representation. If you look then, to those Muslim MPs who were part of Tony Blair's Labour Party, they were pro or abstained on issues to do with war, securitisation and neo-liberalism – and so when I want to consider what the panacea to structural racism and the system's inherent bias against us might look like, I remain unconvinced that it takes place through people that look, sound and have the same names as me, but whose politics are not only alien, they are a complete deformation of my commitment to social justice.[12]

Foster draws on a study which shows that, when companies hired individuals from minority backgrounds who were then in a position to hire, they were in fact less likely to hire other people from minority backgrounds as it was detrimental to their own credibility and standing.[13] Representation can only take us so far, it seems.

Representation within wider consumerism is something I have grappled with too. The right consumer choices allow us to reach the potential that our religion has set out for us. It may not bother anyone that halal food, finance or children's books with Islamic values aren't always easily accessible. But when your consumer decisions are separate from the default options available, it can be hard to feel you are anything but other. You only have to look to headlines along the lines of 'Millions are eating halal food without knowing it', and the debates about whether halal meat should be served in schools to see that consumer decisions by minorities tend to bring about political commentary.[14]

Halal meat has time and time again been used as a political tool. But there is a bigger issue at hand, and it is to do with the brands seeming to cater to Muslim needs: Muslims are only seen as worthy when we are producing wealth. That's why, although David Cameron said in 2008 that giving sharia law official status in the UK 'wouldn't strengthen our society – it would undermine it', adding that 'state multiculturalism' allowed and encouraged people to 'live separate lives, apart from each other and apart from the mainstream',[15] in 2013 he announced a £200 million Islamic bond that would be sharia compliant.[16] The Chancellor of the Exchequer, George Osborne, considered this to be part of the British government's commitment to becoming the western hub of Islamic finance.[17]

For such a long time, the Muslim consumer has been synonymous with the woman who lives a life of indulgence in the Middle East – best illustrated when Dolce & Gabbana released their £3,000 *abaya* range in 2016. Make no mistake, the wealthy Muslim consumer is one that brands (be it Selfridges or Harrods) and governments have always courted and recognized. We will have halal nail varnish, we will have a Muslim family in a Tesco Christmas advert and an imam in an Amazon advert, because the outcome is wealth generation. But when the outcome is real equality, real inclusiveness, or meaningful in any way, we are no longer permitted at the table.

So what sort of representation do I want to see? I've been writing this piece over Ramadan, and so far MAC has produced a 'Get Ready For Suhoor' advert, Nike has released trainers inspired by Ramadan, and MuslimGirl. com founder Amani Al-Khatahtbeh has appeared in a Maroon 5 music video alongside Somali-American politician Ilhan Omar. My first reaction to the music video was, really?! Do we really need representation in music videos? But why was my reaction to Amani being in a music video so different from my feelings about the music of Malaysian singer-songwriter and fellow hijabi Yuna, or even the appearance of Ilhan Omar? Perhaps because Amani has built a brand on her Muslim identity, whereas Yuna's brand is first and foremost her music, and Ilhan Omar's her political career; in the same way that footballer Mo Salah probably didn't set out to achieve Muslim representation in football but became known for his faith as a by-product. The reception of Amani's appearance in the video for 'Girls Like You' was much like that of Noor Tagouri being interviewed in *Playboy*: it was met with some calling it out as misconstrued representation while others were excited at this groundbreaking step. But who gets to draw up the guidelines on what kind of representation is and isn't OK?

Often, Muslims feel like the 'wrong' Muslims have been given a platform, or that Muslims have stepped onto the wrong platforms – be it music videos or *Playboy* magazine. Whether it is Abdul Haqq on Channel 4's *Muslims Like Us* or Saira Khan speaking about extremism, Muslim communities have had clear markers as to who *isn't* the right person to be speaking about our issues. But who *is* right is still something that lies in murky waters. For me, the diverse nature of Muslim communities ultimately means there will never be one figure we'd be happy to see representing us. Representation will always come in bits and pieces, and those representing will not all look like me or be cut from the same cloth. We also need to understand that one person's whole existence cannot seek to represent us. Perhaps I was also unsettled when I saw Amani in the Maroon 5 video because, only a couple of months back, she rejected an award from Revlon because their ambassador was Gal Gadot. At the time, Amani said:

> Her [Gal's] vocal support of the Israeli Defense Forces' actions in Palestine goes against MuslimGirl.com's morals and values. I can't, in good conscience, accept this award from the brand and celebrate Gal's ambassadorship after the IDF imprisoned a 16-year-old girl named Ahed Tamimi last month, an activist who is currently still incarcerated.[18]

It was her moment of speaking truth to power, and I found it enormously moving. And then, in June 2018, Amani appeared in the 'Girls Like You' video alongside Gal Gadot. But the truth is, I cannot expect that everything Muslim women in the public eye do will resonate with my own ideals of what I want to see in the world. In expecting so, we are in danger of contributing to the perception of Muslim women as a monolith by picking and choosing people who we feel represent us and then dropping them when we feel they no longer serve our ideals of representation. We must realize that the critique of Muslim women in the mainstream is often an extension of misogyny and Islamophobia. We all know that if a Muslim woman took part in some of the scenes that Muslim actor Riz Ahmed appears in, she would not be afforded the same treatment and heralded for her acting in the way he has been by the Muslim and wider communities. Nadiya Hussain is frequently the subject of Islamophobia, but it's a very particular gendered Islamophobia. We must be careful that our critique does not demand that Muslim women retreat into silence for fear of being reprimanded.

What we need in our representation will always be fluid based on our context and our changing politics. Someone like Stormzy, who shares my values and my belief that we should seek to speak truth to positions of power, does more to represent me than a Muslim fashion blogger, despite the fact that others might assume that I would have more in common with the latter. At the same time, why should I even draw a comparison between Stormzy and a Muslim fashion blogger? But I do draw that comparison, and that's because, if someone builds a brand based on their Muslim faith, we feel entitled to critique them because we are tied to them by Islam, and not only have they built themselves from the support of the Muslim community but their platform has in part contributed to how Muslims are represented in popular culture. We know that, even if they're totally different from us, the rest of the world sees them as representing us.

It increasingly feels as though the representation of Muslims has been relegated to an identity devoid of faith. That identity is assumed by people like Saira Khan or Amina Lone when it is in their interest to speak on issues that ultimately pit them as 'the good progressive Muslim'. More recently we saw Sajid Javid employ this very tactic when asked about Islamophobia in the Conservative Party: 'For a start let's just look at who the Home Secretary is in this country. As you just described me, my name is Sajid Javid. I'm the Home Secretary in this country.'[19]

Javid implied that, because he had a Muslim-sounding name, it meant that there were no barriers to entry into the party. Suddenly the Conservative Party was apparently being absolved of Islamophobia by a man who had previously been on record saying he was not a practicing Muslim.[20] Similarly to the 1 per cent corporate feminism that Dawn Foster writes about, he used his personal story as evidence that no barriers to Muslims existed. The fact that someone who is not Muslim feels that they can use Muslim identity as a political means to combat accusations of Islamophobia is highly problematic. And let's not forget, stripping the faith out of Muslim identity is also why brands feel that they can muscle in and represent Muslims, as well as have an influence on what Muslim identity should look like.

The diversity amongst Muslims makes it increasingly difficult to sing from the same hymn sheet on where and why we should be represented. To me, being Muslim is steeped in my faith and practice of Islam; to someone else it may be found in their cultural background, or it may be a political statement, or just something that comes to light twice a year at the Eid celebrations. In order for our faith to stay intact in the public and private spheres, we must have guidelines on representation, but where do they come from? Of course we can say our guidelines should come from Islam, the Quran, the *sunnah* and scholars, but with such diversity of faith and practice, who gets to draw up the blueprint? And does that blueprint mean that we – in fact – do not need to be represented in every space and in every moment? A part of me feels like a Muslim conservative Grinch for wondering if I really want to see Muslim women represented in pop music videos, but if we have no guidelines, no points of difference, no sense of having some barriers that we must not break, where does that leave our faith and the status of Islam in today's society? If being Muslim is about faith, the representation of Muslims should come with terms and conditions.

1 'Muslim women's segregation in UK communities must end – Cameron', BBC (18 January 2016), https://www.bbc.co.uk/news/uk-35338413

2 Grayson Perry, *The Descent of Man* (London, 2016), p. 17

3 Yasmin Mogahed, 'A Woman's Reflection on Leading Prayer', http://www.yasminmogahed.com/2010/12/19/a-woman%E2%80%99s-reflection-on-leading-prayer/

4 'More people called David and Steve lead FTSE 100 companies than women and ethnic minorities', *Independent* (18 March 2018), https://www.independent.co.uk/news/business/news/women-ftse-100-gender-discrimination-pay-gap-board-representation-chief-executive-a8244361.html

5 Afia Ahmed, 'How the Turban Hijab Became a Symbol of the Modern Muslim Woman', Amaliah (2 July 2018), https://www.amaliah.com/post/40756/turban-hijab-became-symbol-modern-muslim-woman

6 'L'Oréal makes history by casting hijab-wearing model in hair campaign', *Independent* (19 January 2018), https://www.independent.co.uk/life-style/fashion/loreal-hijab-hair-advert-model-amena-khan-muslim-beauty-blogger-ardere-cosmetics-a8167331.html; 'Why Amena Khan is the Perfect Fit for L'Oréal Paris's New Hair Campaign', *Vogue* (14 January 2018), http://www.vogue.co.uk/article/loreal-paris-elvive-campaign-amena-khan

7 'Amena Khan quits L'Oréal campaign after Israel backlash', Al Jazeera (23 January 2018), https://www.aljazeera.com/news/2018/01/amena-khan-quits-campaign-israel-backlash-180123064327233.html

8 Yassmin Abdel-Magied, 'I Tried to Fight Racism by Being a "Model Minority" – and Then It Backfired', *Teen Vogue* (28

September 2017), https://www.teenvogue.com/story/fight-racism-model-minority-yassmin-abdel-magied

9 'Stormzy doesn't need to be "grateful" for his upbringing as a black Londoner on a council estate – and neither do I', *Independent* (26 February 2018), https://www.independent.co.uk/voices/stormzy-british-black-london-council-estate-grime-theresa-may-government-grime-a8228776.html

10 Dawn Foster, *Lean Out* (London, 2016)

11 'Why corporate feminism is convenient for capitalism', *Guardian* (12 December 2013), https://www.theguardian.com/commentisfree/2013/dec/11/corporate-feminism-capitalism-womens-working-lives

12 Asim Qureshi, *A Virtue of Disobedience* (London, 2018)

13 Stefanie K. Johnson and David R. Hekman, 'Women and Minorities Are Penalized for Promoting Diversity', *Harvard Business Review* (23 March 2016), https://hbr.org/2016/03/women-and-minorities-are-penalized-for-promoting-diversity

14 'Millions are eating halal food without knowing it', *Daily Mail* (8 May 2014), http://www.dailymail.co.uk/news/article-2622830/Millions-eating-halal-food-without-knowing-How-big-brand-shops-restaurants-sell-ritually-slaughtered-meat-dont-label-it.html

15 'Cameron steps into Sharia law row', BBC (26 February 2008), http://news.bbc.co.uk/2/hi/uk_news/politics/7264740.stm

16 'David Cameron to unveil plans for £200m Islamic bond', *Guardian* (29 October 2013), https://www.theguardian.com/money/2013/oct/29/islamic-bond-david-cameron-treasury-plans

17 'Government issues first Islamic bond', HM Treasury (25 June 2014), https://www.gov.uk/government/news/government-issues-first-islamic-bond

18 'MuslimGirl's Amani Al-Khatahtbeh Won't Accept Revlon's Changemaker Award', *Teen Vogue* (16 January 2018), https://www.teenvogue.com/story/muslim-girl-amani-al-khatahtbeh-revlon-changemaker-award

19 Sajid Javid, interview with Andrew Marr, *The Andrew Marr Show*, BBC One (3 June 2018), http://news.bbc.co.uk/2/shared/bsp/hi/pdfs/03061801.pdf

20 'Politics in the pulpit', *The Village* (22 April 2010), http://villageonline.co.uk/village/news/fullstory/politics_in_the_pulpit

The Clothes of My Faith

Afia Ahmed

Belonging is a human need; it is a desire to be accepted and to feel part of a people or of something bigger than oneself. For many Muslims, it is a feeling with which we can seldom identify. We find ourselves more ostracized than ever, like strangers roaming this world with no place to call home. Subject to an ethno-religious penalty, we are never enough; never good enough for here and never good enough for there. And whilst we hail from all four corners of the globe, we find our countries steeped in disarray and our sense of belonging further out of reach than ever before. And because of this need to belong, to feel included, to feel accepted, and to have a voice, we have exerted all our efforts into securing representation in the countries we reside in. It is a representation we thought would lead to inclusivity, acceptance, liberation, and comfort. But did it work and if so, at what cost?

The 'hijab' (usually understood as a head covering) and 'veil' (a face covering), terms often used interchangeably and excessively by people who either observe neither or have negligible 'association' with them, have frequently been refracted through a prism that sees

Islamic beliefs as regressive, constituting oppression and violence. And it is these very items of clothing that have come to define millions of Muslim women, me amongst them. What we once wore as an affirmation of our faith, as an act of submission to God, has become excessively politicized and has come to represent far more than religious observance.

And that goes both ways. Viewed as a symbol and marker of Islam, the hijab and veil are now increasingly worn by Muslim women to reassert their socio-political and cultural identities and act as an affirmation of their ethno-religious selves. In the wake of negative media representations that have made the veil synonymous with terrorism, linking Muslim women to perpetrators of heinous terror attacks and resulting in 'gendered Islamophobia', there has been a backlash: both the hijab and veil have come to signify an anti-colonial struggle and submission to something other than the hegemonic power structures in place in the countries we have adopted. Now, in some quarters, the hijab is a symbol of defiance.

The continual and heated debate surrounding Muslim women, their clothing, what it signifies, and whether it 'belongs', occupies the tongues and pens of plenty – yet the more it is discussed, the less hope I have of progression and comprehensive acceptance. I used to wish dearly to be represented in the fashion industry. I wanted to see someone that looked like me on a billboard, on a television advert, in a magazine; anywhere except on the front page of a newspaper with the headline, 'Veil teacher link to 7/7 bomber'.[1] But as they say, be careful what you wish for. There has been a Muslim boom in the fashion and beauty industries, and we Muslim women have become the West's new 'hot topic'.

Having identified us as a consumer market with considerable disposable income, retailers are lining up to make clothes that fit into the guidelines and framework of our scripture. And you'd think that was fantastic, wouldn't you? But Muslim women are being lobbied for representation in an industry that, as it turns out, continually does nothing to address the class, race and gender inequalities plaguing society and from which Muslims suffer. In fact it exacerbates those inequalities: though we make a great visual, any deviation from popular politics, beliefs, and the image of the moderate Muslimah results in alienation from those who supposedly wish to work with us. We wanted to see better representation, but when we got it we didn't use it in the right ways. We should have forced the focus onto politics, economics, how to improve our parent countries, how to ameliorate the concerns of the working classes in Britain, how to address the attainment gap in education, how to break down the 'Muslim penalty' in the labour market, how to address domestic violence in pockets of different communities. Instead we lobbied, and then we settled.

In a bid to be included and represented by the fashion industry, Muslim women are increasingly sexualized and objectified, and the tenets of our faith have been both appropriated and commoditized. The idea of an essential Islam is being lost as we desperately try to reclaim a narrative about pluralism, individual experiences and insights. As we have fought vehemently not to be regarded as a homogeneous group or monolith, we have forgotten that there is still a standard that we need to live up to. We've allowed Islam to be reduced to 'what Muslims do' as opposed to Islam being submission to God. Muslim women have become the object of the debate, no longer dictating the terms of our engagement and only ever listened to or considered when our religious commitment rests in a liberal paradigm. Muslim women have fought for comprehensive acceptance, yet the only way Western society is willing to engage is within a framework of cultural choices, and when it comes to the fashion world, we find ourselves in a place that expects us to leave behind certain elements of our religion and to comply with a reformed and acceptable version of it.

On our journey to finding belonging, we have left behind those Muslim women who do not see their faces or their outward appearance being represented and who still feel like social pariahs. With a barrage of beautiful, slim, Eurocentric-featured women dominating our social media feeds, dressed in gorgeous clothing and 'breaking stereotypes', we have unwittingly contributed to the separation of the privileged and underprivileged woman. Where we live, our upbringing, our experiences, and our contextual backdrops all have a part to play in what we identify with and what we believe represents us, and these factors likewise shape our reaction to certain industries. I worry that we've contributed to this dichotomy of the fashionable, modern, 'liberal' Muslim woman, versus a supposedly regressive, traditional, 'conservative' Muslim woman. And having more representation in industries as fickle and superficial as beauty and fashion further reiterates that in order to be accepted by society, we have to conform to and fit its beauty ideals. We have to be fashionable, we have to wear make-up, we have to be pretty and on trend, and women who aren't like that, who choose not to wear make-up or subscribe to certain fashion trends, are relegated to the sidelines, to their homes and behind closed doors, to be further racialized and stigmatized – and not just by the media, but by us as a community too. This reality, as unfortunate as it is, extends to all women – Muslim and non-Muslim alike – who choose not to subscribe to, or fail to live up to, fashion and beauty ideals.

The fashion and beauty industries don't have space for all of us; there is only room for the attractive, palatable, and fashionable Muslim woman, and the other is not just excluded, she is vilified. On the one hand we have a wealth of magazines advertising a glorious and heavily made up Muslim woman, and on the other, wilfully misinterpreted images of Muslim women are being promoted by Russian bot accounts, Britain's most widely circulated newspapers are sporting headlines calling for a 'national debate about banning Muslim girls from wearing veils in public',[2] and the head of Ofsted is proposing a ban on headscarves in schools.[3] So when the idea of banning the headscarf and veil is confined to the dustbin of history, when legislation stops policing the Muslim community for religious observance, when Muslim women – both traditional and non – are equally and fairly represented, then I'll buy into the idea that there is tolerance, diversity, and holistic acceptance of Muslim women.

As a Muslim woman who observes both the headscarf and the *jilbab*, I have to say that I rarely see Muslim women like me represented. And before Dolce & Gabbana, Tommy Hilfiger, and whoever else are supplied as evidence in the case against – for their *abaya* catwalks – unfortunately (or maybe fortunately) I don't constitute the 1 per cent who can afford designer Islamic wear, nor do I live in the Gulf states. It strikes me as ironic that while it is Islamic clothing, Islamic culture, and Islamic ideals that are supposedly being represented, the models on those catwalks are not Muslim, the designers are not Muslim, and even the audience present is not Muslim. Similarly, basic Islamic ethics are going ignored; brands continue to exploit individuals working in sweatshops around the world, paying them abhorrent amounts for long and unjustifiable working hours; up-and-coming Muslim designers are not empowered or raised up, nor are they employed to design 'Muslim-friendly' attire (because let's face it, modest doesn't automatically mean Muslim and vice versa). So no, I don't take kindly to my religion and ideology being co-opted and appropriated as a money-making scheme. I do not take kindly to aspects of my religion suddenly being acceptable, and not only tolerated but celebrated, only when a tall, white model is dressed in my ethno-religious attire. I do not take kindly to being told that only when Western fashion deems it acceptable and worthwhile, will I be allowed to showcase and wear my religion proudly on my head and back. Islam has been made into a brand, and I am no part of this brand.

Representation in the beauty and fashion industries has done nothing for productive progression; rather it has fetishized the hijab and taken away from its true meaning. Seeing the hijab being showcased in industries that quite literally profit from creating insecurities in women, and objectifying and sexualizing them, is cognitive dissonance at its finest. Ideally the hijab mitigates instances where a woman is valued solely on her appearance and sexuality – though whether it successfully does that in such hyper-sexualized societies is a whole different discussion – rather it aims to place worth on her intellect, her actions, her character, and so forth. And I truly believe there is much wisdom behind this. It recognizes how fickle we humans can be, and that there is not one fixed idea of what physical beauty is. As Muslims, we take pride in our appearance, but when we become slaves to how we look, we run into a number of issues that by their nature are not meant to be solvable, for if they were, how would these industries benefit?

The other danger in the fashion industry's casual 'acceptance' of 'modest fashion' is that it breeds a false notion of tolerance, which in reality is far from existing. It seems that we have become naive in assuming that because there is some minor industry representation, suddenly Islam is being accepted in its entirety; for its veil, its burqa, its different interpretations in dress, its five pillars, its ideas, and as a system overall. We've forgotten that we're just another number; a target market for sellers on the 'modest' high street. We've forgotten that the hijab is not supposed to be a fashion statement or an expression of choice and freedoms to appease a secular-liberal audience; hijab was and is supposed to be an expression of faith and Muslim identity – that's where it began, and that is where it was supposed to end.

But as 'modernity' envelopes us, we find ourselves struggling to say proudly, 'I wear hijab for me and my Lord, not for you, not for him, not for her, not for them, but for me and my Lord alone.' We find ourselves trying to categorize our decision by placing it in a framework that negates the idea of Islam entirely – a framework that believes religion to be contingent, merely a set of histor- ical practices and rituals, that believes in a complete separation of religion governing our affairs; the idea we stick to because our religion dictates our way of life. The hijab being reduced to a simple head covering – a fashion statement before it is an act of observance – has diluted its meaning and left some Muslim women battling with their *nafs* and spiritual belonging. Granted, many wear the hijab for different reasons, and for some, the hijab becoming fashionable has made it easier to wear. And we also know that some people begin their journey with hijab through a fashion lens; yet it is not fashion that underpins the wearing of the hijab. With so many differing realities, consequentially an identity crisis is quick to catch up, and we find that we now have two unattainable standards we need to live up to; the Western beauty industry and the spiritual level we wish to reach.

And yet. When I think of my baby daughter, I picture her little face looking anxiously at dolls, and finally dancing with glee when her eyes fall on one with a headscarf. No doubt some Muslim women have found confidence and empowerment where there was once ridicule. In a climate where young women are constantly battling identity crises, finding representation, even superficially, can improve things. Diverse representation of backgrounds is important in an industry that supposedly reflects the demographic of the people, and having hijab-wearing women featured in beauty and fashion is not entirely oxymoronic. Yet still, the flaws and the nature of the industry haunt me, and undoubtedly haunt most mothers and daughters of all races and religions. What if my daughter does not fit into society's idea of Muslim female beauty – what if she isn't tall enough, or slim enough, or pretty enough? What if instead of feeling empowered, she feels more insecure?

Before pictures of hijab-wearing Muslim women were everywhere, I was far more confident about not wearing make-up or sporting a plain hijab. I now feel the complete opposite; enslaved by the new Muslim woman who I'm supposed to look like – a better, skinnier, more perfect version of me. I find myself wondering what people on the tube think about my dress. Does it look frumpy and silly? Does my head look big? Do the bumps on my skin stand out? If only they could see my hair, just a little bit, to see that I actually have some. Maybe if I hitched up my *jilbab* they'd see I'm wearing trousers underneath and that I'm pretty stylish. But no, I am just the frumpy hijabi on the tube, supposedly beaten into covering myself in this sweltering heat, a mute with no voice and no brain, indoctrinated by an extremist ideology and with no opinion of my own.

When I first opened up about my struggle with my hijab, someone asked me whether I still prayed – that question broke my heart. My entire faith was being called into question simply because I was struggling with one aspect of it. But I suppose in a way, it made sense. I wasn't supposed to categorize my obligations into more compulsory or less compulsory. If I wanted to practise, I should try my utmost to fulfil all my *faraa'idh*. But at the same time, it made me hate the modest fashion industry, because until my early twenties I had never questioned wearing my hijab. I had never questioned my love for it, I had never hated it even in the slightest – but here I was, scouring the web to find myself a ruling that permitted me to take it off, knowing full well that such a thing did not exist.

When this struggle first began, I felt I had no one to turn to. On one hand, people would tell me that it was a personal journey so I should take my hijab off until I was ready, and others told me I was committing a grave sin if I didn't stick to it. But neither of these was enough; I knew I wanted to keep it on even if I wasn't enjoying wearing it. I didn't believe that I had to justify my struggle through a secular lens and relegate my religion to the backburner. I wanted to continue wearing my hijab, and the only reason for this was because I believed I had submitted entirely to my creator and if it was what He wanted, then it was what I wanted. But it was hard. It was hard because I found I was caught between different communities, wandering between camps and increasingly disliking both. I loved my religion and I hated those who were making me question its beauty. My own choice to wear the hijab had been politicized and commercialized to the point where I didn't know what to do, and for this I blame an industry that consumes women, creating insecurities where there were none. Today the only solace I have found is through contemplation and reflection on the words of God – and His reassurance has been enough for me:

And He found you wandering and guided [you]— Surah Duha, 93:7

Your Lord has neither forsaken you nor has He become displeased. And surely the hereafter will be better for you than the present [life]. And soon your Lord will grant you, and you shall be well pleased—Surah Duha, 93:3–5

Have We not expanded for you your breast? And We removed from you your burden which weighed down your back. And We exalted for you your reputation. Then, surely, with hardship comes ease: surely, with hardship comes ease. So when you have finished [with your immediate task], still strive hard, [then toil,] and to your Lord turn [all] your attention—Surah Inshirah, 94:1–8

As Muslim women, we are all different. And whilst some will read what I have written and nod along, the words on the page echoing the thoughts circling in their mind, others will shake their heads with considerable force, roll their eyes, and toss my words to the side. And that's fine. I'm not here to speak on behalf of all Muslim women.

What I am here to say, however, is that in the recent past, fighting for Muslim women to be able to own their faith and have confidence in Islam was a small battle to be won. Now it has turned into a full-scale war against a global industry intent on creating and fuelling insecurities in women across the world, regardless of their faith. In attempting to secure representation and break stereotypes, we inadvertently find ourselves playing straight into them. It was once argued that we were slaves of the East, subjugated and dominated by the patriarchy, needing liberation and a saviour, but we have since become slaves of the Western fashion world, bound by the shackles of beauty, sexuality, and a desperate need for acceptance.

We have witnessed the creation of a new normative version of hijab, one that is acceptable, tolerable, and digestible. Nevertheless, it is important to remember that whilst we sit in our comfortable homes here in the West, happy at this new representation on catwalks, we forget that ordinary Muslims are being detained, tortured, and massacred by the very governments whose acceptance and approval we so ardently seek. Similarly, whilst we may be happy with some form of representation in the media, there are thousands of Muslims nationwide who are suffering at the hands of class inequality, leading impoverished lives, steeped in disadvantage as government austerity tightens its grip on them.

Many interpretations of Islamic dress are still shunned, including the *jilbab*, the *salwar kameez* (until, ironically, we saw it modelled on a white woman for H&M, who added an extortionate price tag for a staple form of clothing), and the veil, and it is the women who choose to dress in these garments that are often ostracized and maligned. In order to have all forms of the Islamic dress code accepted, we need to reject the idea of hijab being a racial depicter as opposed to a religious garment, and we need to recognize the Arabization of Islam, i.e. the view that anything Arab is Islam or that Islam is everything Arab. Covering is not a foreign concept, and so we need to stop allowing for the internalization of hijab as 'brown' and 'Eastern', which falls directly into the hands of racists and Islamophobes and allows for the successful othering of hijab and, more broadly, Islam.

Contrary to what we are presented with, there is not one type of Muslim woman. There are millions of us occupying our own spaces, changing our own worlds in our own small ways, contributing to what we believe to be the greater good. Fighting for the rights of the minorities within the minorities and seeking representation in industries that value us for more than how we look. And to all those who wish to include Muslim women, a word of advice: if you want to make us feel included, stop singling us out. If you truly believe it is not about the burqa, prove it and stop talking about it. It is not the duty of Muslim women to have to educate entire nations about boundaries, choices, and representation, and neither is it our duty to justify what we choose to wear.

To end, a small message to all Muslim women: I implore you to have confidence and stand tall for what you believe in. You are not what the media tells you to be. You do not have to watch your religion become racialized. You do not need to contribute to the dichotomy. You do not need to pander to the beauty and fashion industries. You do not need to doubt your identity or your origins. You are more, and you will always be more. Remember that we are only travellers, just passing through; but the mark we make will be written into history forever. So here's to the end. I look forward to joining hands with you in the final abode when we get the only representation worth seeking, in the eyes of the All-Seer, the Most Merciful.

Islam began as something strange, and it shall return to being something strange, so give glad tidings to the strangers.—*Saheeh Muslim* hadith, related by at-Tirmidhi, Ibn Majah and Ahmad, 145

مُذَبْذَبِينَ بَيْنَ ذَٰلِكَ لَا إِلَىٰ هَٰؤُلَاءِ وَلَا إِلَىٰ هَٰؤُلَاءِ

Wavering between that [and this], [belonging] neither to these nor to those

—Surah Nisa, 4:143

---

1 'Veil teacher link to 7/7 bomber', *Daily Mail* (21 October 2006), http://www.dailymail.co.uk/news/article-411748/Veil-teacher-link-7-7-bomber.html

2 'Britain needs "national debate" about banning Muslim girls from wearing veils in public', *Daily Telegraph* (15 September 2013), https://www.telegraph.co.uk/news/politics/10311469/Britain-needs-national-debate-about-banning-Muslim-girls-from-wearing-veils-in-public.html

3 'Government should set policies on hijabs in schools, Ofsted chief suggests', *Daily Telegraph* (7 March 2018), https://www.telegraph.co.uk/education/2018/03/07/government-should-set-policies-hijabs-schools-ofsted-chief-suggests/

Life Was Easier Before I Was Woke

Yassmin Midhat Abdel-Magied

When the opportunity arises to be part of an anthology of essays by Muslim women, it's impossible to resist the call. Our cups are overflowing with life to explore but there are so few occasions to do so wholly on our own terms, that to squander the chance would be folly. Yet, the prospect presents an unanticipated obstacle. When writing as a Muslim woman among other Muslim women, one is no longer bound by the broad, representative, generic sentiments so often expected of us and that, despite our best efforts, we often find ourselves sticking to. Being among peers asks us instead to delve into the granularity of our experiences as Muslim women beyond the obvious. In some ways, the obvious conversations are the easy ones. We know what is expected, and what an audience unfamiliar with nuanced perspectives of Muslim women will be comfortable with. Though that narrative is achingly tired, alternatives are few and far between. The space we are allowed to take up is so limited, it leaves little room for the ribbons of our voices to unfurl.

With that in mind, I have decided to take this opportunity to not talk to an 'issue' per se, in the same way

I usually choose to, when speaking to a non-Muslim audience. Instead, I'm interested in meandering through my personal journey as a Muslim woman in a non-Muslim (and often a non-female) world. Because, I am the holder of an unpopular opinion: things were a lot easier when I wasn't woke. Or perhaps they were easier *because* I wasn't woke.

What was easier? What am I talking about? Well, perhaps to explain, we need to take a few steps back. Let's set the scene.

My name is Yassmin Midhat Abdel-Magied, of the Hassan Bey Abdel-Moniem family. I was born in the year 1991, in Khartoum, Sudan, as the city was reeling from its most recent (and most recently successful) coup. By 1992, my family had made the move to a small city in Australia: Brisbane. Faiza and Midhat, my parents, were part of a wave of educated Sudanese that had left their nation due to the change of government. My parents' move, though new and life-changing for our particular family, was nothing unique. We were part of the quintessential migrant phenomenon: the search for a new life beyond a repressive post-colonial regime.

My family were one of the first few Sudanese in Brisbane, and with that came privilege: we were a 'founding family' for the North African migrant community. A number of things reinforced that position of privilege: our early arrival, Mama and Baba's thriving in a system not built to support them, and qualifications that included an advanced diploma, two undergraduate degrees, four Master's degrees, and a PhD (*mashallah*!). Although we may not have been afforded traditional positions of authority and esteem within broader mainstream society, we were creating new traditions and developing a sense of belonging in a new home. Unbeknownst to us, that is one of the ways communities and individuals heal from intergenerational trauma. By taking an active role in defining who we now were, my parents were creating a blueprint for my brother and me to follow: you can choose how to live your life, even when you are completely different from the norm. The method was simple: *Don't pay attention to your difference. Do what you want to do.*

I absorbed this slightly naive lack of self-awareness and in essence, it became armour. I truly believed that I was an equal in all the spaces I entered. Being female, a migrant, an African and a Muslim meant I was often the only one deviating from the norm in a room. And yet I believed that all the stereotypes, biases and assumptions associated with those identities were irrelevant to me. That is why, when, during university, I decided my dream was to work in Formula 1, it seemed like an entirely plausible endeavour. I found people's excitement about the novelty of it all quite humorous. And anyway, my ambition bore fruit: I was accepted onto an exclusive Master's in Motorsports programme and offered work experience at Mercedes F1 in the UK. Unfortunately, the pesky reality of unpaid internships nipped that dream in the bud, and so I found myself back in Brisbane; the possessor of a first-class honours engineering degree and a virtual Rolodex of contacts in the motorsport world, but no income stream and, despite my best efforts, none in sight. The answer seemed obvious and within my control: get a job on the rigs.

I knew I wanted to work on Australia's oil and gas rigs from the day I saw the stall at my university's careers fair in my first year of study. As a budding mechanical engineer, it appeared to combine all my loves: enormous equipment, adventure, travel. Four years later, when the time came to apply for that 'real job', I emailed the man I had met at the fair and asked if his company had any positions for someone like me: smart, accustomed to working with their hands, willing to travel anywhere in the world. My heart leapt when his reply included an invitation to an interview.

'You know you're our first female field engineer?' my new boss said to me at the end of the interview. We were sitting across the desk from one another, and he'd just offered me a job. I nodded, unfazed. Cool . . . ?

'Do you need any . . .' He hesitated. '*Specialist equipment*, seeing as you're a woman?' His thick Glaswegian accent did not hide his discomfort, though I wasn't sure why he would be feeling that way. I laughed in response.

'Yeah, I mean, do you have women's clothing? I hate having to fit myself into men's trousers, they don't really work for my body.'

My manager's face creased into a frown. He clearly wanted to show support but didn't actually have the capacity to follow through on any request I might have. I picked up the standard men's uniform a few days later.

The second conversation of this sort happened on the drive to my first rig, my colleague behind the wheel.

Earl looked at me out of the corner of his eye. He opened his mouth to start a sentence, then closed it. A moment later, he tried again. No sound.

'Earl, are you OK?'

'Yassmin . . . listen. I've never worked with a woman before.'

Again, I laughed. These men were so worried! What for?

'I mean . . . we work with pretty heavy equipment. Are you going to be able to . . . lift the tools?'

I looked at Earl, throwing some of the shadiest side-eye I've ever thrown. I'd been going to the gym and lifting weights since I was twelve years old. I'd held the bench press record for my age group at school. I was much, *much*, larger than Earl.

'Earl . . . You're a Filipino man half my size. I can lift *you* up!'

Earl smiled, uncomfortable and tight lipped, then fell silent.

I looked out of the window at the desert passing by, my eyes unfocused, the conversation almost completely forgotten. This was going to be fun, I thought. I can't wait to show them how wrong all their assumptions are!

I had no reason to believe that I should be treated any differently from my co-workers, no reason to think that my experience in the workplace would be any different from my life in school and university. Boy, was I wrong. The rigs were a different world. During my undergraduate studies, the power dynamic between my peers and me was fairly even. Ultimately, I was competing with my fellow students on grades, and I'd spent enough quality time with professors, tutors and classmates to create the human-to-human connections needed to overcome any bias and prejudice they may have had. At work, however, who I was came with no inherent power. I was a young, female graduate in a hyper-masculine working environment, and a clear deviant from 'the norm'. It was becoming obvious that there was a chasm between my understanding of my place in the world and the reality of it. Here, on rigs in the middle of the desert and ocean, my process of awakening would begin. This change would take time

Anne Summers, a prominent Australian feminist, once said to me that *young women don't think they need feminism until they have a child*. The implication was that having a child is a life stage when the difference between women and their male colleagues becomes irrefutable. The conversation occurred a number of years ago, before feminism enjoyed the resurgence in the popular consciousness that it's going through today. Her statement bore some truth, but in my case, it wasn't having a child that spurred my belief in the cause. Rather it was my entrance into a space where my gender was inescapably obvious and so unarguably different from the accepted norm that something was going to have to change. To nobody's surprise except my own, the environment I moved into didn't change; I did. I fell into the pattern of so many female engineers before me, who did what they could to survive.

Research by Deneen M. Hatmaker at the University of Connecticut published in 2013 shows that women in engineering tend to fall within two main categories when dealing with the male dominance of the workplace: coping mechanisms and/or impression management.[1]

Internal coping mechanisms include 'blocking' and 'rationalizing': blocking involves using verbal blocks of any kind to stop any mention of gender or gender identity. This serves the purpose of bringing one's professional identity to the foreground, and attempts to prevent any gendered biases, expectations or stereotypes affecting an interaction. Rationalizing is a more cognitive process whereby female engineers convince themselves that they're 'OK with' unfair or discriminatory behaviour. Importantly, these techniques help with coping (they help the engineer – me – feel better about the situation), but rarely change long-term behaviour in any substantive manner.

'He's an old man, of course he would say that about women,' I'd say to myself. 'Oh, they didn't mean it like that!' 'They're teasing me because I'm now part of the group.' 'I'm not like other girls, I can hack it!' 'It's no big deal . . .'

I fell into the rationalizing category, hard. It was easy to do: when trying to fit into a group, where you're the only one who is 'different' and when your income is dependent on being accepted, there is an enormous amount you can rationalize to yourself. It also helps if you're unaware of the biased dynamics at play. Only in the years since I left the rig have I been able to consider – and admit to myself – that some of the behaviour I encountered was unprofessional and inappropriate at best, and sexual harassment at worst. At the time, I was able to rationalize almost all of it away.

Impression management, the second category of survival strategy, I also used in spades. The two techniques within impression management, according to Hatmaker, are 'proving oneself' and 'image projection'. Both of these are 'external facing' strategies that try to influence the perception of others. Proving oneself is as simple as it sounds: being *so good* that you outperform your gender, or, ostensibly, your entire identity. The ultimate achievement is to be recognized as a technical expert. On the other hand, image projection involves women typically choosing to project a 'gender neutral' version of themselves. Hatmaker did identify some cases that provided hope: when impression management embraced 'gender ownership', the women were coping by owning their gender and projecting positive aspects of being a 'woman engineer'.

This, of course, is the most successful strategy in the long term. Women feeling comfortable enough to project an image that being female is *positive*, where it is currently seen as a negative, or at best neutral, can only be beneficial. However, it requires a lot of work – internally and externally. 'Identity work' is an extensive and exhausting process, and many women – and any group that doesn't enjoy the power and individuality of being in the dominant demographic – are doing this work at all times. It is no wonder that the retention of female employees in STEM (science, technology, engineering and mathematics) is dismal: after twelve years, 50 per cent of women in STEM will have left their jobs, compared to 20 per cent of women in other professions. Most of those leave in the first five years.[2]

It's much simpler to navigate a world that you believe is level, and where your individual actions define the opportunities you have to progress and succeed. It gives you a sense of power, and control. Choosing to see otherwise – to think of yourself operating within a system that sees you as a sum of one-dimensional, inferior identities – can be, and often is, overwhelming. So, I resisted.

I pushed back against the idea that I might be faced with racism, sexism or discrimination. Look at my privilege, I would say. My education, my class, my lightness of skin tone. If people pointed to the specific experiences of others, I believed that I could continue to do what I had always done: rise above. Naivety, arrogance, or an unexpected blessing in disguise? Either way, the belief took root because I *wasn't aware*.

I was unaware of the impact of history on my current existence. I was incognisant of the systemic inequalities that exist. I was ignorant to the cunning adaptability of the system, which learnt to use the example of the exception to make liars of those who dare shine a light on the true nature of the rules. Oh, how I believed! I was curious, but not curious enough: I had yet to entertain the thought that I should *never* need to earn my equality. I was starting from a basis of believing that I needed to earn my right to be seen as equal. A heartbreaking admission, in hindsight. But alas, we all start our journeys into consciousness at different points, and my time was fast approaching.

I distinctly remember the moment I began to realize 'gender ownership' was an option for me, marking the beginning of my journey of awakening. At the time, I was a year and a half into working as an operator on rigs in Western Queensland and the South Australian desert. It was hot – temperatures above 40°C were typical – and grittily dusty. Insects thickened the air, colliding into us and each other with pure abandon. I was sitting next to a colleague of mine in our 'donga', a refurbished shipping container that doubled as our office while we were on site. My colleague, an old friend from university, was a jovial and straightforward character. Although I was in a supervisory role on site, our relationship was friendly and collegiate.

Our conversation had turned to a comment one of the men had made about me, somehow referencing my gender. I couldn't tell you what the remark was; all I remember was being furious that he kept mentioning the fact that I was a woman.

'Why do you get so mad anytime anyone mentions that you're a chick?' my mate asked, abruptly. 'Like, I mean – you are one, right?'

I nodded, unsure where the conversation was turning. My forehead creased as I tried to parse the meaning behind his words.

'Well, why don't you just, I dunno, embrace it or something? I mean, I don't know what it's like to be a woman, but surely there are some advantages to it? Why don't you, like, just focus on them?'

The question stunned me. Bizarrely, I had never thought to see my gender as an inherent advantage before. Paradigm-shifting moments don't often come in a neat package, yet mine came in the form of a simple question from a Measurement While Drilling operator on a rig in Western Queensland. It planted a seed: perhaps I didn't need to think of my difference as something needing to be compensated for. I could be proud of my difference, wholly and fully. In a way where I wasn't confined by borders drawn by others, but where I took ownership and chose to define the space I wanted to take up myself.

As I would later learn, this idea was dangerous. Fully taking up space, in a way where my equality was not conditional on good behaviour – oh! This belief would lead me down the most difficult path I'd ever walked.

As for the details of that story? Ah . . .

A simple Google search will give you the basics of what happened to Yassmin Abdel-Magied in 2017. I had, up until then, been the Model Minority™, but with a single Facebook post I suddenly became the Controversial Muslim Activist™. To say it was a shock to the system would be like calling Hurricane Katrina 'a bit of a breeze'.

Mine was a virtual public lynching, constituting a Murdoch-press character assassination and months of attack by the conservative government, ostensibly on the basis of my identity as a Muslim migrant. And I faced it without the backing of my employers, my university, or any of the major organizations for which I had volunteered or that had given me awards over the years – the very same institutions that had benefited from my Model Minority™ performance to date. The people who did have my back were the creatives – writers, artists – those who were already awake.

For me, 2017 fed the seed of change planted on the rigs with steroid-infused fertilizer. The kernel grew into a thick stem of understanding, irrevocably transforming my conception of the world. You see, although I'd had a paradigm shift with respect to gender, I had yet to apply that perspective to other facets of my identity treated with bias: faith, migration status, race. It took losing everything – my public standing, my job, my safety – to fully comprehend the scope of the lesson I had learnt.

I could no longer accept the conditional equality that I had been socialized to be grateful for. I would accept nothing less than substantive, transformative and unconditional equality, for myself and for others. If we are equal in the eyes of the Lord, how can anyone allow otherwise? This was what I would now fight for, until my dying day, *inshallah*.

Once you have begun the journey of awakening, there is no turning back. Your eyes have been opened to the ways of the world. These are forces not easily unseen.

With the burden of knowing comes a freedom, bittersweet. At least, it did for me. The pressure to be enough: gone. The pressure of earning equality: lifted. I realized by accepting this reality I had unknowingly centred somebody else's rules, instead of following my own. My rules are those of my faith, and they require me to answer to nobody except the Almighty.

Sweet, these freedoms, yes. But the aftertaste is bitter, because in order to undergo the process of change, one needs to recognize and name the problem. Constantly doing that is exhausting. Engaging with and understanding the structural nature of inequalities in the world is crushing, and it's not just the weight on one's shoulders. Sometimes it feels as if my very bones are heavy; the marrow weighed down with lead. Truth has turned my soul's light spirit into the viscous tar of molasses. Opening your eyes to the light can help you see, but it can also blind you. That is not the fault of the light, but our bodies can only carry so much, and our eyes cannot continue to see without blinking.

And so, I search for the middle ground. Seeing, with the respite of the blink. And my journey is not nearly complete. I am not entirely 'woke', for that would mean a finished product, which I am far from being. I am on a journey of awakening to the world around me; a constantly evolving project taking into account where I have come from and where I might, *inshallah*, go. That's why the space to talk about different realities for Muslim women is so important. Our lives are not uniform. My story is not representative; it is simply my own. It is not a reflection of anyone else's truth. It does not cancel another's pain or want to be seen as more than what it is. Mine is a single person's lived experience. An experience full of contradictions, imperfections and incongruities, but my lived experience nonetheless. Part of the journey, for me, is owning these inconsistencies in myself and my stories – we cannot change our past perspectives, but we can certainly reflect on them, own them, and commit to growing from them. We must cultivate compassion for our past selves, trusting that we did the best we could at the time, while simultaneously striving to do better.

I did say it was easier, back when I wasn't woke. I didn't say it was right.

1   Deneen M. Hatmaker, 'Engineering Identity: Gender and Professional Identity Negotiation among Women Engineers' in *Gender, Work and Organization* (2013) 20:4, 382–96

2   'What's So Special about STEM? A Comparison of Women's Retention in STEM and Professional Occupations' in *Social Forces* (21 August 2013), 92:2, 723–756, https://academic.oup.com/sf/article-abstract/92/2/723/2235817

'There's No Such Thing as a Depressed Muslim'

Discussing Mental Health in the Muslim Community

Jamilla Hekmoun

The first time I had a panic attack I thought I was going to die. Seriously. I was ready to say my *shahadah* (declaration of faith) because it felt like my life was coming to an end. I have been anxious for as long as I can remember, but while I was living abroad during my second year of university, things got much worse. At the time, I did not even know it was a panic attack; I thought I had a heart problem. I had woken up with my heart racing and feeling an overwhelming sense of dread, like something horrible was coming. I had just turned twenty and was on a year abroad in Amman, Jordan. I was thousands of miles away from my closest friends and family and I felt alone, and afraid.

When our mental health is good, we are supposed to be able to handle the normal pressures of everyday life. But what is normal? Normal for one person is not normal for another. I now know what is normal for me, and when things are abnormal I know I must seek help or make an extra effort towards self-care. After that first terrifying panic attack in my new home in Amman, I went to hospital and found out that my condition was stress related. Until then, I had no idea that stress could manifest so dangerously. I had always been told that everyone gets stressed and that I should not make such a big deal out of things.

It is unfortunate that mental ill health is often not taken as seriously as physical illness. Part of the problem – no doubt – comes from the fact that everyday life is full of triggers that can affect you, and you alone (for me, a mindless scroll through social media can tip me into sadness), and, of course, there is no single example of what mental healthiness looks like. But there is a societal problem at the root of our attitude towards mental illness too, and it's a problem that is particularly prevalent in the Muslim community.

I was lucky compared to a lot of other Muslims who suffer with mental illness. I had received a relatively secular education in regard to mental health, and so, after talking to friends who confided in me about their own diagnoses, I eventually went to the doctor. It was only after that appointment, once I had a name for what I was going through, that I started researching Islamic ways to cope with my emotions. But when I looked online, on social media and Muslim forums, I was struck by the overwhelming prevalence of one single idea: that you could not be Muslim and depressed, because a true Muslim would be content with what God had planned for them.

A key idea within Islamic thought is that Islam offers its believers totality; that it can provide solutions. But that attitude can result in a very black-and-white view of mental health. And it leaves those who are suffering entirely on their own. It's a problem that others have recognized. Inspirited Minds is a charity I have volunteered with since 2016, and it was established in 2014 to answer a need for a faith-sensitive mental health organization. Inspirited Minds promotes an understanding of mental health through an Islamic lens, as well as offering practical solutions to mental illness that are in line with Islamic thought. Studies have found that Muslims are often reluctant to get help regarding their mental health as they face stigma from both within the community and outside it.[1] Muslims are often afraid that they may experience Islamophobia when seeing non-Muslim therapists and practitioners, particularly because that therapist may not understand the role of faith as either part of their problem or part of the possible solution. Within the Muslim community, there is often a lack of acknowledgement of mental health issues, but many also fear judgement. In Islam, alcohol, drugs and pre-marital relations are all forbidden, as is suicide. Therefore, when a Muslim whose mental health issues are tied up with one of these turns to the community, they often find nothing but judgement, when what they seek is the relief promised by the Islamic principles of mercy and forgiveness.

But there are other contributing factors to the stigma surrounding mental health. Pride and familial honour are hugely important in the Muslim community, and no one wants to feel as though they are bringing shame to their parents by admitting they are suffering. Many of the elders in the British Muslim community are first-generation immigrants who had to struggle every day just to make ends meet, and many refuse to see mental health illnesses as legitimate because of the prevailing attitude that the best thing to do is to 'get on with things'. Unfortunately, another response that many in the Muslim community have towards mental health issues is to blame jinn. Jinn are spirits, invisible beings, which live in a parallel universe and are capable of possessing humans. They have had a strong presence in many South Asian and Arab cultures through history. It is easier to ascribe mental health issues to black magic or the supernatural rather than look at entrenched problems. The solution? Extra prayers or more fasting.

While religious practices may offer help in some ways – be that as distraction or a space to practise mindfulness and meditation – they often do not combat the root of the issue, and in some situations they can exacerbate the problem. For example, if a Muslim has an eating disorder such as anorexia, then encouraging them to fast, even during Ramadan, can be potentially dangerous. Another issue is scrupulosity, a form of OCD linked with anxiety where the sufferer is fixated on obsessions to do with their religion – for example, in strong and excessive feelings of punishment and inferiority, and increased compulsions to try and get rid of these obsessions. The compulsions could be repeating prayers, fasts or other religious rituals multiple times because of fear they have been performed incorrectly. Needless to say, offering prayer as a solution to this form of OCD can be enormously detrimental. Religious leaders and mental health practitioners need to understand the complexity of mental health disorders in terms of the sufferer's religion; a one-size-fits-all approach does not work.

I wish I could say things got better when I returned to the UK from my year abroad, but the following year, they worsened. My father and younger siblings had moved to war-torn Libya, and the constant worry and news of the death of relatives sent my anxiety through the roof. I remember being unnaturally attached to my phone, having it with me 24/7 because I thought that I was going to be called with news of death or destruction. A few years later and my phone is still my safety blanket – I carry it with me at all times, though I know it is just down to leftover anxiety that I think something bad is happening.

I am not unique in this experience, though. Most young Muslims in the UK are the children or grandchildren of immigrants from South East Asia, Africa or the Arab world, and we still have family or connections in those countries. Many of these nations are experiencing war, famine or disaster, and the consequent worry about what our family, friends and fellow Muslims are going through has a huge impact on our mental wellbeing. And it's worth underlining the importance of the latter. Muslims are constantly being reminded that we are all one *ummah* – that we are of one body, and when any limb aches, the whole body reacts with sleeplessness and fever. Therefore, the trauma of one Muslim community is felt the world over, by each and every Muslim. And the British Muslim community is experiencing a lot of tension. We live in the most deprived areas of the country and make up over 13 per cent of the prison population.[2] There is a high number of Muslims in social housing and we have low levels of full-time employment. We have less money and less access to services than the general population, and even something as trivial as our names can stop us getting employed.[3] These stresses impact on our mental health – how can they not?

Sometimes it can feel as though the whole world is against the Muslim community. Islamophobia in the UK is increasing,[4] and the dehumanization of Muslims through physical or verbal abuse feels almost constant. When there is a Muslim perpetrator of a terrorist attack, anti-Muslim sentiment and Islamophobic attacks increase, and the consequences of those attacks can be felt throughout the Muslim community, resulting in conditions such as agoraphobia, anxiety and post-traumatic stress disorder. These stresses may not be understood by the non-Muslim population, but it is something that impacts Muslims on a daily basis, and that's why mental health needs to be taken seriously in the Muslim community – because there is an increase in conditions exacerbated by societal factors. The need for faith and culturally specific mental health support is increasingly important.

A frequent sentiment we hear in regard to mental health issues from many in the Muslim community is that someone is experiencing depression, or suicidal thoughts, because their faith is low. They are not praying enough, or they are being ungrateful and not thinking about how lucky they are compared to other people around the world – the 'well, you cannot be sad because other people have it worse' argument. Not only are these arguments dangerous, but they are also invalid in Islam. There is a *hadith* about someone who asked the Prophet (pbuh) whether he should leave his camel untied and trust in Allah that it would not be stolen or run away, or if he should tie his camel (*Sunan at-Tirmidhi*). The Prophet (pbuh) replied that he should tie his camel *and* trust in Allah. So, Islam encourages us to take both practical *and* spiritual approaches to problems. I remember going to my local imam when I was first diagnosed with anxiety, as I was confused about whether or not to take the medication that my GP had given to me. He said something which has resonated with me ever since. That, if I was in physical pain, there would be no question about taking medicine to get better, so why should that be any different with a mental illness?

My imam was right. The sentiment that mental health issues stem from a lack of faith is in fact both incompatible with Islamic thought and practices, and historically inaccurate. Muslims have a rich history in contributing to psychology, or, as it is often referred to in Islamic thought, *ilm an-nafs*, which translates as the knowledge or science of the self. It is the medical and philosophical study of the mind from an Islamic perspective; one which incorporates the Quran, the *sunnah* and Islamic tradition. It is about the psychological concepts rooted within Islam, which have been fostered by the knowledgeable within Muslim history. Ibn Sina (Avicenna), Al-Ghazali and Al-Kindi were all pioneering Muslim thinkers who paved the way for mental health treatments and aimed to remove the stigma surrounding them.

I have had varied responses from the Muslim community when discussing my anxiety. When I first started writing about my struggles and about mental health in general, I had a series of negative reactions from fellow Muslims, and even some of my friends. I remember one saying that he thought there was no such thing as mental health, whilst others associated good mental health with religiosity; the more pious you are, the more well you will be. I have had Muslims tell me that all I need to do is complete extra prayers to be mentally healthy.

But the emphasis on prayer as the sole solution can be hugely problematic. Prayer for Muslims is personal, and everyone has different experiences and a different relationship with it. Generally, it is a compulsory ritual undertaken five times a day, every day. It is one of the five pillars of Islam and central to the Muslim faith. Many will say it is the defining factor of what it means to be a Muslim as it represents the constant remembrance of a higher power. Before each prayer, one must be ritually clean, and a process called *wudu* (ablution), which involves washing certain sections of the body, is undertaken. It means being absent of physical impurities as well as a spiritual ritual of preparation. But to define prayer as simply a ritual would be to ignore the connection that many feel when talking to, and thanking, God. Prayers usually take up to ten minutes each and comprise that small section of the day when Muslims can escape their daily lives and connect with God. While many Muslims see this as relaxing, and as a chance to seek comfort, for some Muslims with mental health issues, it can be a daily struggle. To find the motivation to pray – or to do anything – can be difficult when you are suffering from mental illness. But when other Muslims see that you are not praying, regardless of the reason, they can be extremely judgemental.

It is important to have an open and honest conversation about prayer when you are experiencing mental health difficulties. Whilst prayer is important to Muslims, it is only one element of the Muslim faith and only part of what recovery involves. I think it is a subject that needs to be taken seriously but also handled with kindness; because sometimes, to be honest, it can feel as if you are barely able to keep yourself alive, let alone keep up with your daily prayers. There are days, and I have had them, when your mind becomes so clouded, and your body and brain feel numb yet under intense pressure. It is as though you might burst. You can barely get out of bed, you forget to eat or drink, and there's no way you are capable of prayer. But being told that you are a non-believer for not being able to pray regularly makes things a lot worse. You start thinking, well, if I am so bad then there is no point in me trying to pray, and if I can't pray, then am I even Muslim?

My imam made me realize that having a mental illness did not mean I was not a Muslim, and that it was a combination of spiritual and practical solutions that would help me to recover. As bad as things have been for mental health sufferers within the Muslim community, things *are* changing for the better. It is a step in the right direction that Muslim mental health organizations such as the Muslim Youth Helpline and Inspirited Minds offer training sessions for imams and community and religious leaders, because I've no doubt that we need more imams like mine; imams who are ready to explain that it is not about choosing either a medical solution *or* a purely spiritual one, but about integrating the two. He wanted me to ensure that my emotional and mental health was a priority. And that also helped me to see how prayer would help me. Knowing that my mental illness didn't mean I was un-Muslim, knowing that praying didn't have to be the only solution, meant I could see what it could offer me. After all, we are Muslims: we do believe in an all-powerful, all-healing God that can help us through our troubles. Even when I have been so low that I cannot get out of bed to kneel on the prayer mat or to make ablution, I have found that just sitting and making *dua* can be comforting.* When at my lowest, I found that prayer offered me companionship, because even though I felt alone, I still had God to talk to, and I knew He was listening.

It has been over two years since I finally got help, and things are still mixed. I know I have people to talk to, and that is comforting, but there are many days when

---

*   Different from the five daily prayers, a *dua* is a prayer that can be said at any time, without the need for ablution or special clothing.

it feels like the world would be better off without me. Sometimes my depression has such a hold on me that I cannot think clearly. I want to do anything I can to distract myself from it, so I dig my nails into my arm or leg. The physical pain is easier to deal with than the mental because there is an end in sight. With mental illness, you cannot see an end. When it all gets too much, and I cannot cope, it makes it hard to sustain my faith. It took me so long to realize that experiencing this does not make me a bad Muslim. Struggling is a part of our faith journey, and I have tried to use my faith as an aid to my positive mental health recovery. Even if I am not able to pray, I try to take a few minutes out of the day to sit quietly and recount to myself that I do believe in a higher power, that I believe there is a God who wants the best for me and that when I have no one else to talk to, I can sit and relay my troubles to Him.

It can take a lot to accept that you have a mental illness. When I was diagnosed I was terrified of what it meant. Was I crazy? Would my friends and family think differently of me or treat me differently? Did it mean God was not pleased with me and wanted to punish me? I think this is something every Muslim who has ever been diagnosed with a mental health disorder goes through. But my mental illness does not define me. It might change my mood at times, but it does not change who I am, and, most importantly, it does not make me a bad person, especially in the eyes of God.

Verily, in the remembrance of God do hearts find rest.—Surah Ar-Ra'd, 13:28

---

1 'Mental health therapy for Muslims embraces religion', BBC (12 February 2017), http://www.bbc.co.uk/news/uk-england-38932954

2 Dr Sundas Ali, 'British Muslims in Numbers', report prepared by the Muslim Council of Britain (January 2015), https://www.mcb.org.uk/wp-content/uploads/2015/02/MCBCensusReport_2015.pdf

3 'Is it easier to get a job if you're Adam or Mohamed?', BBC (6 February 2017), http://www.bbc.co.uk/news/uk-england-london-38751307

4 'Islamophobia in the UK increasing, Tell MAMA report claims', Sky News (2 February 2017), https://news.sky.com/story/islamophobia-in-the-uk-increasing-tell-mama-report-claims-11109524

Feminism Needs to Die

Mariam Khan

Islam is a religion that empowers women. And yet, for many young Muslim girls, their understanding of Islam comes entirely from a series of cultural interpretations of their faith dictated by the patriarchy. With this and the lack of conversation within their communities about women's rights, the first time many Muslim girls in the West will encounter female empowerment is likely to be from a White Feminist perspective. But there is a problem. This perspective disapproves of the hijab, the burqa, modest culture and other key elements of the Muslim female identity. Mainstream feminism suggests that my choices and values can't exist within its framework – if I make the decision to dress for my faith then I must be oppressed or submissive.

Before I go any further, I need to explain exactly what I mean by White Feminism, and how I'll use that term for the purposes of this essay. White Feminism (which is still the mainstream) centres the agenda and needs of white, straight, middle-class, cis, able-bodied women while making claims that it speaks on behalf of all women. White Feminism doesn't recognize that my identity as a Muslim and a person of colour (PoC) cannot be set aside in the pursuit of equality for 'all women'. So when I say White Feminism or White Feminist in this essay, I'm not simply pointing out the colour of someone's skin (if I'm doing that, I won't be capitalizing the 'w' of white) – a White Feminist is someone who furthers that ideology no matter who they are.

In my first year of university, I studied feminist theory. That was my first time really being educated about women's rights and empowerment. I grew up in a Muslim community whose cultural understanding of Islam denied equality of the sexes and rarely left room for female voices, let alone female empowerment. The community centres, associations and mosques were filled with men and run by men. As a child, I remember not being able to go to prayers in the mosque because there was no space for the women; the men had expanded into it. Their space was non-negotiable and sacrosanct; ours was free for the taking.

But that's not to say the women in our community were willing to be silenced. We created unconventional spaces for ourselves. For a few years, on some Saturdays we'd attend a small gathering at the house of an auntie who had organized for a female preacher to come and talk to us all about the Quran, to help us understand our faith, and to bridge the gap between our cultural understanding and what Islam really was. We'd find out when these meetings were happening by word of mouth, during chats outside the school gates, or – if we were lucky – via the odd landline call the evening before to confirm, yes, there was a meeting on. Thinking back now, this felt like a small revolution. Muslim women piled into a living room whenever the message went out. Whenever we went, Auntie's house would be bursting at the seams, shoes and slippers gathered in mismatched piles outside her front door, as so many sisters and mothers came to listen to what their faith said about them. Mum couldn't drive back then, so we'd walk and were always the last to arrive. We'd squeeze through the bodies packed together in the small room, trying to avoid stepping on hands or feet or babies, the words of the female preacher humming over the microphone someone had had the foresight to invest in. I learnt very little because she preached in Urdu, but what I did understand from that experience was that Islam made space for women. I just didn't yet know what to do with that information.

Later, as I sat in my lectures and began to understand what feminism was, to realize that my voice could matter, that there was a movement where women were encouraged to speak up, I was reminded of those Saturday mornings. Except this time, the conversation was happening in English; I understood what was being said and if I didn't, I could ask. Suddenly, there was an answer to the frustrations I had felt growing up in a community that had long since intertwined patriarchal culture and religion. There was a label that I could use which allowed me to act on the things I believed women should have: the right to an education, to equality, to having a choice and agency. I was a feminist and defining myself in this way sparked something inside me: a need to understand the rights I had as a Muslim and the rights I had as a woman, and if they were compatible. I would come to know that, although Islam allowed me space to explore this compatibility, feminism refused it.

Though, in my earliest years identifying as a feminist, I didn't realize I would come to a crossroads, it was always difficult balancing my two identities. Islam wasn't making it difficult, but feminists were. Every time someone asked me, 'Are you a feminist?' and I replied, 'Yes, I am,' they would instantly question me: 'But how, aren't you a Muslim?' All the while, they were eyeing my hijab, probably imagining how it was thrust upon me each morning. How could I know what feminism was if I subscribed to a faith that they believed oppressed women? How could I be a feminist? Feminism for White and mainstream feminists has been about many things, be that #freethenipple, period poverty, the freedom to wear revealing clothing, the freedom not to wear high heels to work, shared parental leave or the fight for equal pay. As a woman who lives in the West, all of these things are important to me too. Though I don't wear short skirts and I really dislike wearing heels, I will fight for the right of women who want and deserve to have autonomy over their bodies. But somewhere near the beginning of my journey into feminism, I realized that this entire sisterhood of feminists, this global movement, wasn't as committed to me as I was to it. The feminism I saw would only stand up for a specific group of women. Women like me, who were beyond this core group, were on their own.

Now I have come to that crossroads. I am a feminist, but I'm not sure feminism is for me. Would those with whom I fight in solidarity fight in solidarity alongside me when I need them to? I know the answer is no. Many times, I've been disappointed by so-called feminists. And many times, the groups and women I have identified with have rejected me: the way I look, the way I dress and the faith I practise. Without even trying to understand the intersectionality of my identity, they have dismissed it, and in doing so they have dismissed me. I'm tired of being asked about the way I choose to dress as a Muslim woman. I'm tired of answering 'so when did you start wearing it?' and 'did your parents make you?' and 'will you make your daughter wear the hijab?' and 'what if your daughter doesn't want to wear hijab?' These questions, disguised as curiosity, are underlined by a silent and persistent 'but are you sure it's your choice?' Those people are looking for ways to tell me I am not a feminist. Those people want to tell me how oppressed I am. Or they are desperate to squeeze me into their understanding of what a 'Muslim Feminist' should look like: they tell me I am different from more 'conservative' Muslim women, that I am 'liberal' and 'moderate' – words that pull me into a narrative that they perceive to be acceptable.

Every White Feminist I have come across will argue until they are blue in the face that women should have the right to decide how to dress themselves. And then those same people are unwilling to stand up for a Muslim woman who wears a hijab or burqa because they 'don't believe in it' or 'feel like Muslim women are oppressed'. They can't entirely explain or point to the oppressor. Neither can they acknowledge that they themselves are playing the role of oppressor by impressing their ideology of empowerment on others who may interpret empowerment in a different way. So I've found being a feminist taxing because I am so emphatically othered in a movement that should represent all women. The terms of my empowerment as a woman are dictated by what White Feminism and the West perceive as empowering.

Being let down by White Feminists is nothing new. In 2012, Caitlin Moran interviewed Lena Dunham, the creator of HBO's *Girls*, and after the interview Caitlin was asked on Twitter if she'd addressed the lack of people of colour in the TV series. Self-proclaimed feminist Caitlin Moran proudly responded, 'Nope. I literally couldn't give a shit about it.'[1] I was at university at the time, and up until that point I had thought Caitlin and I were on the same team: she was a feminist and I was someone who'd newly happened on feminism. But I was wrong. So long as Caitlin's white privilege served her, equality for all women be damned. But the thing is, a woman of colour or a Muslim woman in her position could never not 'give a shit about it' because their colour and their faith are not things they can separate from their identity as women. I am a woman, but I am also a Muslim and a person of colour, and these identities cannot be separated. I can't set aside being a woman of colour when it comes to being a feminist and I can't set aside being a Muslim woman when it comes to being a feminist.

More to the point, I will not set it aside.

Somehow within feminism there is an expectation that faith needs to be left at the door. I'm so tired of conversations about how 'Islam treats women', when in actuality the person lecturing me doesn't even know how Islam says women should be treated. They don't know that the rights feminism has granted them, Muslim women had from the beginning of Islam: women like me had the right to vote, to own property and wealth, the right to an education, and the right to work centuries before western feminism jumped into action. When I point this out, many will bring up the niqab or the burqa as examples of how the clothes of my religion are oppressive, and yet it isn't permissible in Islam to force the niqab or the burqa upon Muslim women. What we wear for our God is a choice for the individual. Isn't feminism about choice above all?

Even when Muslim feminists attempt a discussion between themselves, that conversation is co-opted by Islamophobes and White Feminists. The conversation around periods – how we talk about them, whether we disguise them and how much they should cost us – rarely acknowledges Muslim women, but come Ramadan, the Islamic month of fasting, all of a sudden everyone is interested in us and our menstruation. In a recent conversation about periods and Ramadan, I was asked why Islam is ashamed of and encourages Muslim women to hide their periods. The cultural patriarchy exists both within the Muslim community and outside it, and I have many friends who aren't Muslim women who will take a 'sick day' because of cramps. I don't know a single woman who will tell their male manager that it's period cramps that are hampering their work, and women who need to borrow a paracetamol or a sanitary towel hardly shout it across the office. Islam clearly indicates that during Ramadan Muslim women who have their period are exempt from fasting because Islam recognizes the toll it takes on your body. Islam does not shame women or their periods. And it doesn't ignore them either. I have the same cultural frustrations as every other woman fed up of hiding their period, but the moment I was overheard expressing these frustrations to another Muslim, someone else redirected the conversation to focus on Islam and the way it is perceived to oppress women, neatly reinforcing a narrative that is present in the West.

In a piece for the *New York Times* titled 'Being a Feminist in Harvey Weinstein's World', *Big Bang Theory* actress Mayim Bialik wrote, 'As a proud feminist with little desire to diet, get plastic surgery or hire a personal trainer, I have almost no personal experience with men asking me to meetings in their hotel rooms,' further explaining, 'I dress modestly.'[2] Though my logical mind does not want to believe that such a well-educated woman believes 'modesty' is a deterrent to sexual abuse and sexual abusers, she is in fact saying exactly that. Well-meaning feminists are often the people who perpetuate an exclusionary feminism that centres their experience as universal. Feminists of all stripes were quick to condemn Bialik for victim-blaming, and she subsequently apologized for the piece,[3] but that doesn't change the fact that 'modesty', a word often scorned and sneered at when used as part of the Muslim female narrative, was now being proposed as a defence from sexual abuse – as if Muslim women who dress modestly have never been sexually abused. It's not even that Muslim women aren't being allowed a space in this conversation – it's that time and again conversations like these push Muslim women (and women of colour) outside the female narrative altogether. The discussion around a movement as big as #MeToo – which, remember, was started by Tarana Burke, a black woman – has since been co-opted by White Feminism and well-meaning white feminists who will easily exclude an entire group of women based on the assumption that dressing modestly somehow protects them from sexual harassment or assault. Shortly afterwards, the well-known journalist and feminist commentator Mona Eltahawy shared her story of being sexually abused whilst being on Hajj in Mecca. She started the hashtag #MosqueMeToo and thousands of Muslim women followed her example and shared their experiences of abuse. Backlash came from Islamophobes and bigots who used these stories to further demonize Muslim men. A conversation that should have been completely centred on Muslim women and their trauma was once again co-opted by outsiders with an Islamophobic agenda. To compound that, it didn't have the support of the mainstream conversation happening around #MeToo, which seemed entirely focused and solely concerned with the abuse of White Feminists.

The term 'intersectionality', originally conceived by Kimberlé Crenshaw in 1989, discussed the multiple systems of oppression marginalized people faced. In its inception Crenshaw centred race and gender because Crenshaw was a black woman writing about black women. I believe we should all exclusively identify as intersectional feminists; in doing this we are allowing ourselves to recognize how power structures overlap and reinforce each other and how feminism today is dominated by white, cis-gendered, middle-class, able-bodied women who refuse to acknowledge the multiple layers of oppression women of colour have to go through. If White Feminists want to be a part of the narrative they will need to de-centre themselves and their views of empowerment to include women of colour, trans women, non-binary women, gender-queer people and women of faith. Empowerment comes in many forms and oppression shouldn't be defined by what isn't default to a White Feminist's world view. Feminism as we know it needs to die so it can stop building walls, so it can develop and move forward to nurture a sisterhood of Intersectional Feminists. Feminism is no good to me if it doesn't fight for every different type of woman.

During the Women's March on Washington in January 2017, civil rights activist Linda Sarsour gave this speech in front of hundreds of thousands of people, and I felt seen by feminism for the first time:

If you want to know if you are going the right way, follow women of colour, sisters and brothers. We know where we need to go and we know where justice is, because when we fight for justice we fight for it for all people, for all our communities.[4]

And although it is complicated, it's that simple.

1 Caitlin Moran, 5 October 2012, 5.29 p.m. Tweet.
2 Mayim Bialik, 'Being a Feminist in Harvey Weinstein's World', *New York Times* (13 October 2017), https://www.nytimes.com/2017/10/13/opinion/mayim-bialik-feminist-harvey-weinstein.html
3 Lila Thulin, 'Mayim Bialik Apologizes (for Real This Time) for Her Victim-Blaming Op-Ed', Browbeat (19 October 2017), http://www.slate.com/blogs/browbeat/2017/10/19/mayim_bialik_apologized_for_her_victim_blaming_op_ed_on_the_weinstein_scandal.html?via=gdpr-consent
4 Linda Sarsour, speech (21 January 2017), https://www.youtube.com/watch?v=DnaT8JxUTY0

Hijabi (R)evolution

Afshan D'souza-Lodhi

As I am writing this, I'm surrounded by what looks like hundreds and hundreds of scarves piled on my bedroom floor. I'm moving. I've been moving for over six months. Issues with my new house mean that I haven't been able to actually pack up and leave yet, so I've been living out of suitcases and boxes for just over half a year. But, strange as it seems, I'm kind of glad. It gives me time to figure out what to do with all these scarves. These scarves aren't for winter or those tiny fancy things some people tie around their necks to look fashionable. No. These scarves are headscarves – in dozens of different colours, lengths, styles, and thicknesses. I even have a rainbow-coloured one somewhere, for Pride, of course. Some smell of *ittar* and others have that mouldy scent of clothes packed in closed suitcases for too long. I make a note to myself: 'wash scarves before packing them' – if they're coming with me, that is.

I've had an on-again-off-again relationship with my hijab. The first time I wore it – or rather, the first time I wore my approximation of a headscarf, a bright orange tablecloth I'd found lying around the house – I was six.

My mother, my father and I had come to the UK the year before from Dubai, and all I knew was that I wanted to wear a headscarf. I fought with my parents about it. My mother, a revert, had never worn one. I didn't even have any older sisters or cousins who wore one. In fact, in my primary school, there was no one who wore a headscarf. I think my father thought that this sudden determination to wear a hijab was down to religious zeal. I can't really remember. I only knew that wearing it meant that you belonged. I spent the first five years of my life watching hijabi women in Dubai walking around in groups, laughing, talking, and most importantly belonging to something bigger than themselves. I wanted to belong, I wanted comfort, and I wanted a sense of community in this new country. My mother didn't think I understood the reasons women wore hijab, and she was probably right. But this was who I wanted to be. Thankfully, my parents saw that. They gave in. For me, the hijab became a symbol of solidarity.

Throughout my pre-teen years, nothing could deter me from wearing the headscarf: not even 9/11. After that atrocious day, classmates would ask me if Osama bin Laden was my uncle, but I remained unfazed. I thought people were laughing with me, not at me. I was determined to be Muslim, visibly Muslim. Not just any Asian kid, but a Muslim one. As the years went by, my white headscarf became a part of my identity, and I started to take on the religious aspects of Islam in other parts of my life, praying at least twice a day. I became known in my primary school as 'the girl with the headscarf'. My cousins thought of me as 'the weird one who's making us all look bad'. My father loved it. He could turn to all his friends and tell them that his daughter was *so* religious that *she* had decided all by herself that *she* wanted to wear hijab. My mother was less impressed. She saw and felt the racism that wouldn't register with me until I was older.

And then I got to secondary school. A change of school and a change of uniform: I was getting older and my mother decided that I could and should fully understand the implications of my decision. It was only then that I was told about the times people shouted at my mother in the street. When little Afshan was running ahead with a white hijab and an ice lolly in her mouth, strangers would stop my mother and ask her if she had no shame: she was raising a terrorist. Terrorist. That word still haunts me today. Prior to 9/11 it was a descriptor for someone's activities; a person who terrorizes. Post 9/11, the word *terrorist* only meant Muslim; it had become a racialized term. My mother had a different take on my headscarf: she told me that she had issues with how 'good' a Muslim I was. Should I be wearing hijab if I wasn't fully practising? I was, after all, representing *all* Muslims. She understood the power of representation, the hyper-visibilization that follows hijab-wearing Muslimahs around. With hijab, she told me, came a set of rules: there was to be no laughing loudly in public, I must pray five times a day, and I must at *all* times be a model young Muslim woman. My school uniform included a short skirt; my mother and I both agreed that short skirts and headscarves didn't mix. Perhaps it was this, or hearing about the racism my mother had endured, or perhaps I just wanted to make friends without the responsibility of constantly representing a religion – I'm not quite sure. But when the new school term came around, I decided to start secondary school without a headscarf.

Once I got to my predominantly white private school, it dawned on me that I wasn't going to make friends easily anyway. I didn't have many social skills and preferred reading and spending time in the library to sitting on the grass and gossiping. I did make one friend that first year, another Muslim girl, a hijabi. Her attitude towards hijab and Islam would forever change the way I understood the religion. For a year, I watched as she spoke loudly, laughed fully, and even swore. She inspired me to wear the hijab again, and the following summer I chose a new black headscarf to go with my school uniform. I would be starting the new school year as a hijabi. The first few weeks of that term were laughable. Teachers couldn't seem to recognize me, as though they had never actually seen my face, just 'the brown girl with the long hair'. I remember sitting in an IT lesson with the same teacher who had taught me the year before when she turned to the room and said, 'It looks like we have a new girl in the class. Would you like to introduce yourself?' This wasn't an isolated incident. There are only so many times a girl can respond with, 'Miss, it's me, Afshan.' I persuaded the head of year to let me change my school picture. Some teachers just could not reconcile my non-hijabi picture with my hijabi face.

As if being Muslim and having to deal with race and religion wasn't enough, it was around this time that I began to realize that I was bisexual. I had been aware of sex and sexuality (the ways in which people would sexualize me) as something that was mysterious and forbidden, from a young age. I was told to sit upright so as not to let my top gape and to stop playing with boys in case people – read: aunties who would report back to my parents – got the wrong impression. I certainly found boys attractive, and I liked girls too, though until I read about bisexuality, I didn't have a word for it. My 'coming out' was about finding a term that fitted what I already knew about myself. And then I started reading: stories in the media of imams shunning gay people in the UK or killings of homosexuals in Saudi Arabia. I was told, from news programmes I watched with my father or listening to my elders debate, that having 'gay thoughts' wasn't so much the issue; acting on them was the sin, and the Quran only dealt with acts of sodomy. As I couldn't understand Arabic (and therefore couldn't see for myself what exactly the Quran said), I was left to read numerous translations, opinions and writings on the topic. All of them led me to the conclusion that non-heterosexual relations were forbidden. Part of me didn't even want to research further for fear of finding out that, in fact, I could be a sinner simply for desiring. Slowly, my prayers became less frequent: five times a day, twice a day, until I stopped altogether. All I could think was that being gay and Muslim were incompatible. And if that was the case, what was the point in praying?

Despite this, I still wanted to be Muslim. I wanted to be good. I fasted during Ramadan because my family did. I prayed with my parents. But my heart wasn't in it any more; none of it seemed to fit the person I wanted to be. I started to view being bisexual as a vice. I remember making a list of all the things wrong with me. 'Bisexual' made an appearance twice: the first time I crossed it out; the second time, I underlined it. My sexuality was my biggest problem. I wondered if I could will myself to only like men. The internet seemed to think so: 'if you're bisexual, then just don't fall in love with women,' any number of anonymous forums on Islam and sexuality advised. I was only part *haram*: part gay and part Muslim.

By the time I reached seventeen, I had had enough. I took off my headscarf. I was fed up with the racism and hated having to represent Islam wherever I went. Whilst arguing in a philosophy class that not all Muslims were homophobic, I realized I didn't want the burden of representation any more. Wearing the headscarf that labelled me as Muslim didn't allow me an opinion of my own; to others, my opinion was Islam. And apparently everyone knew what Islam was. For the two years that I removed my headscarf, I felt a little freer. Free from Islam, free from representation, and free from having to act in certain ways. I felt as if I could finally be who I wanted to be. Or, at least have the freedom to find out who I was separate from Islam. My religion fell away, only coming into play on dark nights when I cried for the Lord to end it all. Those were the times my head hit the prayer mat, in tears and dreaming of death. During those nights, I felt that I had failed at everything. I couldn't be a proper Muslim, and I couldn't be properly gay. I couldn't even kill myself properly.

University was my attempt at running away from my problems. Unlike other 'good' Muslim girls, I had decided to leave Manchester and go to London to study. My mother and father let me go on one condition: I had to wear a headscarf. For eighteen years, my parents had never once asked me to wear it, but now that I was leaving home, it was their only stipulation. 'It's not that we don't trust you, we don't trust other people,' my father said. My mother just nodded. 'The hijab will protect you,' he said, and my mother packed me some headscarves. So off I went to university, wearing a headscarf. I instantly regretted it. Navigating freshers' week and living in student accommodation as a hijabi was incredibly difficult. Part of me wanted to go out and 'find myself', and the other part knew my hijab had its limitations. The moment I arrived, I was faced with people making assumptions about what I believed and how I would behave, and of course, my mother's 'good Muslim' rules continued to echo in my mind. While all my new friends were going out, giving themselves alcohol poisoning, and having the night of their lives with someone whose name they'd forget the next day, I stayed in my room, being that 'good Muslim', hoping to find solace in online gay forums.

For most people, the queer scene (and by that, I mean the clubbing scene, because until recently a sober queer scene wasn't a thing) was accepting and open. But for a kinda Muslim, fat, South Asian hijabi, it just wasn't. My hijab covered my sexuality. I found myself being ignored in queer spaces, having to be overtly queer to be noticed – dropping hints in conversation and wearing anything rainbow coloured because otherwise people assumed I was in the wrong room. I was constantly told I didn't look queer enough and that I couldn't possibly be queer. I stopped wearing heels and dresses and started wearing military boots and leather jackets, a dress code I thought would allow me to be accepted. The only thing was, my skin colour and religion didn't allow for that. I didn't fit the stereotypes of what a queer woman looked like. I had to drop my use of *alhamdullilah* and *mashallah* and *inshallah* from my speech, exchanging those words for partial lies, introducing myself as '*culturally* Muslim'. I was playing into the narrative that I was an oppressed Muslim girl who just wanted to come out and leave her religion behind.

Slowly, things began to change. Through the gay

forums I came across a group of women I liked and we started going out for drinks. I wore my military boots and a leather jacket, but this time no headscarf. I went by Ash. Not Afshan. I became someone else when I was with them. And for some time, I enjoyed that person. But by the morning, my headscarf would be back on and I'd be Afshan again, just in time for my lectures. My depression returned (in hindsight it hadn't really left) and I turned to anything to help medicate. My daytime hijabi and nighttime 'Ash' nametag, along with sleeping pills, alcohol and whatever antidepressant the NHS had me on, helped me get through the first two years of university.

After two years I made the decision to fully remove my headscarf. I told my parents. I didn't ask them. I spouted something about racism and racist attacks in London, which wasn't a complete lie. But I made it out to be worse than it was. I convinced them that removing my hijab had nothing to do with identity and everything to do with safety and survival. I spent my final year at university as a non-hijabi. At least now I could be 'properly' queer – whatever that meant.

I graduated, just, and got a job almost straight away. Late nights were exchanged for early mornings and I found myself back where I started: in Manchester, living with my parents. When I returned home, my headscarves were still packed in suitcases, alongside expensive books that I would never touch again.

And now, as I prepare to move out of my parents' home, I have dragged those same suitcases out from under my bed, and the scarves lie melting over boxes around me. I see my transition with the different scarves and styles of hijabs I have worn running parallel to my personal journey. I went from wearing a white scarf with my neck showing, to nothing, to a black scarf with my neck hidden, to a longer thicker black scarf held with many pins, to nothing, to multi-coloured scarves and flower bobbles to give me volume, to nothing. Scarves with holes in from where safety pins have pulled the threads beside *dupattas* with necklaces attached. Scarves and materials of different lengths and colours and weights surround me.

Hijab has served me well. At times, it has covered my scars, allowing me to wear long-sleeved tops without anyone questioning what was hidden underneath. Other times, it has served to cover my earphones while I avoided listening to teachers drone on in class. Sometimes, very rarely, it has kept my head warm during cold winters.

My hijab gave me a way to act, a code of conduct: smile courteously at strangers, open doors for people, help the elderly carry their shopping, and politely decline drugs/alcohol/male interaction as they are 'not allowed in Islam'. My hijab was my armour, something for me to fiddle with when people asked me uncomfortable questions. It would allow me to look down and cover the acne growing on my forehead when someone attractive walked by. At times when I was tired or frustrated, I would untie and retie my hijab. Now, I do so with my hair. It's not the same.

The periods of wearing hijab and not wearing hijab didn't exist in isolation. I didn't just wake up one day and become a non-hijabi. There were transition phases. I tried my best not to confuse people, but the sighs of disapproval I received upon removing my headscarf got stronger each time I took it off. At each stage, people who had no business judging my choices had something to say. Wearing it means telling people you are religious and not wearing it means you are not religious any more, they'd say. What they saw was a hijab binary that didn't allow for complex, contradictory people to exist. I was a walking contradiction: a queer Muslim.

I say 'was' rather than 'am' because I no longer see Islam and queerness as oppositions. Islam is peaceful and I have to constantly remind myself that just because people don't accept me, doesn't mean that Islam or Allah won't. I'm not going to supply you with quotes from the Quran or the *hadith* to justify my own existence. You can google those yourself. I've had to justify my own existence to myself for too long. I'm not doing it any more.

Reclaiming Islam as a queer woman has been hard. Islamist terror attacks across the globe mean people shrink when they see brown skin. Attacks in queer spaces and against women mean people wonder what reason I have to wear a hijab now. Why, after all these years of Islamophobic attacks, assaults and racism would I own a religion and culture that seemingly hates who I am? Making *my* faith *mine* has been a journey and a half, and I'm still not there yet. All I know is that if I don't own it, then I'm broadcasting a message of fear. I've lived in fear most of my life: fear when I see a group of white boys throwing fireworks into the middle of the street and wondering if the next one will be aimed at my face, fear of coming home to my mum after a brilliant performance at a queer festival and wondering if she will shout at me, fear of going to hell after waking up from a failed suicide attempt, and fear of not being good enough.

I'm done being scared. If I don't take ownership of my body, my religion, my headscarf and my sexuality, then I'm telling the bigots they have won. I'm done giving power to racists and White Feminists who want to dictate how Muslim women should dress. I'm done engaging in conversation with people who don't understand that human beings are complex. That I can wear a hijab and a dress. That I can be queer and Muslim. That I can exist.

Tomorrow, the next day, and the next, when I'm getting dressed, I will look at myself in the mirror and decide there and then if today will be a hijab day. It looks like the scarves had better come with me.

Eight Notifications

Salma Haidrani

It's 7 a.m. and my phone keeps pinging. It's a sharp trill, indecently loud. Bleary-eyed, I grab it. One eye on the screen, it's too late to think I should have hit airplane mode before I fell asleep. I feel like I'm suffocating the moment I view my Twitter notifications. There are eight. Blue, shiny and unopened.

I might be in my bed but I certainly don't feel safe.

I roll over and throw the phone across the room. *Here we go again.*

I'm scared of my phone. Actually, that's not strictly true. I'm not scared of the cat-shaped case, with blue and white diamonds encrusted on it. The best bit? It saves me time rummaging in my black handbag. When I take a photo, it's often the first thing that people notice. But I am scared of the sounds my phone makes. Where I used to spend languorous lunchtimes scrolling through memes, and where there was once a sliver of excitement the moment I pressed on the blue bird icon, I now dread the number of notifications that might await me.

It wasn't always like this, but since I started writing articles about Muslim women in early January 2016, the number of messages I receive has increased – it seems like everyone has an opinion about Muslim women. The first article I wrote was for *Broadly*, *VICE*'s women's interest channel, and it was a feature on the UK's first halal sex shop. The sex shop was the brainchild of a Nottingham-based businessman who wanted to offer Muslim customers the opportunity to purchase (among other items) gelatin-free lube, vibrators and kegel balls. The catch? There wouldn't be a bacon-flavoured sex toy in sight.[1]

Humorous as it might have seemed on the surface, I was hoping to shed light on the limited opportunities for Muslim women in the UK to explore their sexuality when most mainstream sex shops – which often have sexually explicit store fronts – could be intimidating for them. I hoped that readers would recognize just how far the UK's first halal sex shop, which offered a nudity-free buying experience, could serve to empower Muslim women.

I was the first person in the UK to profile the halal sex shop in depth, and a sense of pride spread through my body when I saw the published article on my screen. So imagine my shock when I returned after lunchtime and logged back onto Twitter: there were many more than eight notifications waiting for me.

Most of them had nothing to do with the article itself. A few didn't even care to read the full piece, posting comments along the lines of 'How can the sex toys be classed as halal? Are they blessed?!' A few times, I reminded them to re-read the article but quickly realized it was all falling on deaf ears. I couldn't quite believe my article could elicit that much outrage from complete strangers.

I blocked several people and tried to push the messages out of my mind but they swam back to the surface. Never mind, I told myself, this wouldn't happen every time I wrote an article on Muslim women. But several months later, in April 2016, I penned a new piece for digital women's magazine the *Debrief*. The article, the first of its kind in the UK, focused on the realities of being a British Muslim woman in the aftermath of a terror attack, and in it I discussed everything from the way Muslim women are expected to shoulder the blame, to our fears of facing anti-Muslim hate crime.[2] This time, the notifications were angry, blaming an entire community for the actions of a few. Within moments of promoting my article on Twitter, someone messaged me to tell me that 'all Muslims are terrorists', and another person tweeted photos of anti-Muslim protests. I was too exhausted to defend myself and deleted the Twitter app from my phone until things calmed down.

I started writing about Muslim women that year for two reasons: I hadn't seen any journalism reflecting the lived experiences of British, liberal, educated and un-apologetically Muslim women like me and, to be quite frank, I was tired of waiting for anyone else to do it. I'd also started to notice how acceptable Islamophobia had become in casual conversation. One close friend had ranted about how excited she was to leave for Australia as 'there were no Muslims there'. After a slew of hateful comments, I plucked up the courage to confront her, unwittingly releasing a mob of like-minded women who picked up where I left off. Safe to say, we're no longer close friends, but it also made me realize how important it was that someone from my community stand up and begin to speak. If ordinary people like her thought I was the 'enemy within' and didn't mind vocalizing it in pub-lic, then what was being said in private? Challenging misconceptions became the focus of my journalism, and that meant I became the focus of some pretty hateful responses online.

The last few years of my life have looked a little like this:

In the summer of 2016, I land an internship at a magazine famed for its youth culture. It's one of the most turbulent socio-political climates in recent history – post-Brexit racism (it's a month since the referendum) has reached a feverish high, and an hour away from the UK, French police are forcing Muslim women to undress on their beaches in the name of empowerment. I've never felt more terrified to be a Muslim woman. Or more visible. I feel hopelessly out of control. When did Nigel Farage become as much a part of the twenty-four-hour news cycle as David Cameron? It's almost as if he's become the prime minister.

I decide to write a photo-led piece about the perspectives of British Muslim women. I name the article 'British Muslim Women Talk About How It Feels to Be Constantly Spoken For'.[3] Not once have I seen a Muslim woman discuss what's going on politically – nor have they been given the platform. Celebrating these women's defiance in the face of Islamophobia and harmful policies that have only served to other them and isolate them from the mainstream is the only thing I can think of doing. Journalism, I'm increasingly realizing, has the power to build bridges between communities in the face of hate and hysteria.

I soon come to learn that there is nothing more satisfying than celebrating women who make readers completely re-evaluate their idea of what Muslim women should 'look' like. Humaira and her septum piercing. Or Anisha in head-to-toe streetwear, looking like she belongs on a Hypebae Instagram post. Persuading them to appear in the article is tough – they worry that I might manipulate their words or that the article will lead to a backlash. Luckily, they're happy for me to take photos of them alongside their quotes. 'Don't speak for me. I'm perfectly capable of speaking for myself. Does that sound oppressed or weak?' one of my interviewees says. It's my favourite line and I scrawl the words onto a piece of paper to keep for myself. I tuck it in my handbag.

Once my article is online, I decide to share it on Twitter. I'm terrified, and log out the moment I hit 'tweet'. For the next hour I can barely breathe. When I do eventually check to see the response, there's a smattering of hate (clearly I'm getting used to this) but it's heartening to see some tweets of support from young girls. One is only seventeen years old. In her DMs, she writes: 'I love your work. I hope you continue to thrive and inspire others as you've done with me.' Another tells me she's come across my work and would love to be a journalist herself. It's the reason I do this, after all: so women like her get the chance to hear from Muslim women, as I never did. Older readers message about how proud they are to see a young Muslim female journalist dispelling myths. I resolve not to feel so anxious about the work I do from here onwards.

Later that summer, the notifications seem to have taken on a new life in my mind, and one morning I wake up drenched in sweat after dreaming that someone has sent me a DM threatening to follow me home. I don't touch my phone for hours.

But at other times, a newfound confidence seems to envelop me. It's surprisingly hot and I've found myself braving a bare leg more often. I write more articles on British Muslims: from their opinions on our new prime minister[4] to their reactions to a YouGov poll finding that 57 per cent of the British public support a burqa ban.[5]

The more women the world over message me about the impact my work has had on them and how it feels to be seen and finally heard, the shorter my hemline gets.

Even so, I'm living on my own for a few months and I'm less terrified of a burglar than I am of a St George's Cross flag thrust through my letterbox. I decide to switch up the times I come back at night, extend that impromptu dinner reservation, stay later at work. I turn down my music on the short walk back from the tube.

A week later, I've changed my mind. I start returning each night at exactly the same time. No head turning to look behind me for fear of a not-so-random knife attack. No lowering my music. I increase the volume of 'Hotline Bling' till my ears are stinging in protest. I refuse to be cowed into fear. I've made the decision to write about this community and if that provokes people, so be it.

It's still August and I'd love to spend the last warm days reclining on the grassy bank of my local park, a Twister in one hand and a chick-lit novel in the other, but I'm at work, Terry Richardson portraits still hanging on the wall above the desks. I'm imagining that I've turned off my wifi and am soaking up the sunlight, the rays hitting my bare legs. I can almost feel myself tilt my head up to the sky, but then an editor is trying to get my attention. 'Do you fancy going to UKIP's London hustings?' he laughs. 'I mean, you don't have to . . .'

I think of one candidate who's spent the whole

summer accusing Muslim women of being submissive. This could be my chance to take her on – and at their final hustings no less. I've got a gig on later but I can skip it. This could be a good story. 'Sure,' I say, as I brace myself for the evening ahead.

At 7 p.m. I find myself at the Emmanuel Centre in Westminster, a stone's throw from Parliament. A UKIP supporter is waving a placard outside, declaring his support for the leadership contender Diane James. Inside, the yellow and purple UKIP colours are emblazoned across the walls. Rows and rows of bald heads are in front of me. I'm surprised that a lot of young men have turned up to support the party too. There I was thinking we were in the midst of Corbynmania.

Five candidates are vying to succeed Farage – three women and two men. Diane's decided not to turn up and as each of the remaining four take to the stage, they use it as an opportunity to make subtle digs at her no-show.

At the mere mention of the word 'Farage', the room is heady with rapturous applause. There's a hushed tone when they say his name, as if it's so sacred that civilians like us shouldn't dare mention it. If we were at Hogwarts, this would be a Slytherin meeting, I think to myself. But this is real life – and a significant proportion of people in this room believe we should close our borders, that Islam hurts women, and that it's OK to vote for a man who deployed Nazi-style propaganda to secure Brexit votes. Knots are tightening in my stomach as people milling around the room look at me, pause and stare.

Someone senior is leading the hustings and briefly stops when he sees me. *What the hell is she doing here?* I can see the words play out in his head.

The post-Brexit result rouses everyone out of their seats, shouting and screeching as one candidate launches into a fervent tribute to Farage. The photographer and I are the only ones sitting down and staring uncomfortably at the floor. It's only been two or so hours but time seems to have stretched. I'm tempted to go to the toilet and vomit but I don't want to draw further attention to myself.

I'm terrified. It's bad enough seeing it in the newspapers, but being amongst people who voted for a party that conflates my faith with 'evil' is a whole new experience.

At the end of the night, I manage to catch the female candidate who's spent her entire campaign lambasting Muslim women. She denies that accusation, using the tired 'from my experience' trope. I manage to catch all of our conversation on my recorder and tuck it away safely so I can file a piece tomorrow morning.

I barely sleep that night. When she spoke, the candidate claimed that Muslim women are circumcised against their will, that they are forced into marriages, and that they want to belong to British society but their faith doesn't allow them to. 'Is this what everyone else thinks about me?' I ponder. Her vile words are circling around my brain. The next morning, I have to relive it all again as I transcribe the recording at my desk. In the background I can hear the Brexit euphoria, the 'taking back our country' screeches, and it feels as though they are enveloping my senses.

'How was it?' the message from my editor flashes up.

'Fantastically vile,' I laugh. I hit the 'send' button once I've filed the piece and find myself able to breathe for the first time in hours.

*

It's mid-September 2016 and I've started noticing how much I used to take my security for granted. At work, I've managed to wander in without a pass for the last two months. No one seems to have noticed it – I barely register a second glance from the receptionist or the employees milling around the black sofas.

'I don't want to get Charlie Hebdo'd,' one male colleague retorts at our morning conference meeting when he's discussing a risky article he's writing. Everyone starts laughing but there's a bitter, brooding energy in the room. I pretend that I'm momentarily distracted by a Terry Richardson artwork hanging on the wall, but I'm relieved that he's vocalized something I've thought of before, that I pushed to the inner recesses of my brain. It's too terrifying to contemplate in its entirety. If I had said something similar, I doubt it would have elicited the same response – for all the strides we seem to be making for women having a voice in the morning meetings at our office, somehow I don't think that a woman of colour saying, 'I don't want to get Charlie Hebdo'd' would be quite as hilarious.

I find out they're building a new security system at work and I sink temporarily into relief. But for a few moments I'm transported; I think about what my obituary would say if gunmen really did storm the place. How would people describe me? I don't think I'm quite the right shade to make it onto the homepage of the *Daily Mail*. I laugh in spite of myself. God forbid what the comments would say if I did – they've got a moderator, but the bile that still seeps through sometimes makes me feel as dizzy as two rounds on a helter-skelter.

*

It's a typical Friday night later that month. My sister is ordering an Uber on my phone and presses the Twitter icon to distract herself.

'You've got new notifications,' she says off-handedly.

'Are there more than eight?' I laugh, waving a mascara wand through my eyelashes. I feel that familiar flicker of panic rise up again.

She's looking at me as if I've grown another head. 'Eight notifications,' I repeat. 'Anything more than eight and it means two things – something you've tweeted might go viral and you'll end up on BuzzFeed forever . . .'

I pause for dramatic effect as one of her eyebrows suspends itself on her forehead.

'Or you've riled them and you're about to be the latest object of performative Twitter rage,' I laugh. The Uber's here.

I've noticed that my behaviour has changed as I've become more fearless with my journalism. Usually I'd turn down any TV appearances for fear of making an error on a catastrophic scale, but when a message from a Sky News TV producer pops up in my DMs, I jump at the chance. They want me to take part in their new free speech feature, 'The Point', where participants have a minute or so to make their point on a topic of their choice. Mine will focus on urging the British public to end the campaign to ban the burqa and how it's time to stop policing Muslim women's bodies.

The car collects me at 7 a.m. *Have I finally made it?* I think as I climb in. I pretend for a second that there's waiting paparazzi and I wave to no one in particular. 'Get a grip,' I laugh to myself as the car whizzes through the sleepy Sunday morning streets. The Sky News building looms large against the horizon.

'So what are you in here for?' the make-up artist trills as she sweeps blusher across my face. She tells me I'm 'brave' when I fill her in on what I'll be talking about. I'm hearing that a lot these days, but I don't like that word too much.

At the last minute, just before we begin filming, I decide to add my email address to my Twitter biography. Perhaps an editor will see me on TV and want to commission me.

The Sky News office is undeniably impressive and I have to pinch myself that I've been invited here. The producer and I make our way to a small windowless room. I'm instructed to stare at a TV screen. 'Make sure you talk slowly,' the producer reminds me. Over my allotted minute, I talk about how Muslim women like me aren't in desperate need of liberating. Believe it or not, we have as much choice as other British women, I remind viewers. Ironically, these conversations are forced on us, yet our opinion isn't once sought, I add. 'Enough is enough,' I end with.[6] The experience is less nerve-wracking than I expected. Though I wonder if I'll be spending the rest of my journalism career reminding people that British Muslim women have as much freedom and choice as our non-Muslim counterparts. I hope not, I think as I leave.

When I wake up the next morning, I have three emails in my inbox, all names that I don't recognize. All male. The subject lines (the first is 'Your Television Appearance on Sky News Today') look like vague threats. I open one. It's almost four hundred words describing all the injustices against Muslim women the world over: from female genital mutilation to forced marriage. He asks why I'm so convinced, then, that Muslim women have so much freedom. Every word is in capital letters and ends, 'I DOUBT YOU WILL RESPOND TO THIS AS YOU ARE A COWARD.' I'm tempted to remind him that this isn't a religious issue – it's a cultural one – but realize that it'll only spur him on if he elicits a reaction. To think someone dedicated time to my TV appearance via an email rant!

I laugh and hit 'delete'. I decide not to read the other two emails lurking in my inbox. Another email arrives and I delete that too, then remove my email address from my Twitter bio. As humorous as I might have found it, it's terrifying that people I've never met can directly contact me. I close my email and recite 'tomorrow's fish and chips paper' to myself several times.

An old friend from university who has moved to Atlanta sees my television piece. He says he doubled over in shock when he realized it was me. I don't think he remembers me as being quite that gobby. Nonetheless, he flashes up on my DMs, saying how proud he is of me. Another mate Snapchats the clip and tells me how he pointed to the screen and shouted, 'I know her!' After all the hate I've received recently, I'm almost in tears to have my views validated. It reminds me that my message – campaigning for the right for Muslim women to be seen and heard on their own terms – can travel across the world.

The leaves are starting to turn brown and my internship is coming to an end. I've been questioning whether I want to stay in journalism. Do I really want to carry on feeling shaky every time I look at my phone? Do I want to live in a constant state of anxiety? Do I deserve to be the subject of angry tweets?

I think back to all the pieces I've written over the past year, a significant number of which are about British Muslims. My coverage is unlikely to get me a job quickly. A 2015 report found that Muslim women were 71 per cent more likely than white Christian women to be unemployed.[7] A reassuring statistic, I tell myself, as I embark on newfound unemployment.

On my last day at the magazine, I look at my bank account and inhale sharply. For the first time I wonder whether it was all worth it. No one plans to take a vicious beating online and then pay the price by skipping lunch. It's not as if the effort I'm making in dispelling myths and humanizing women like me instantly converts to a tuna baguette.

But then I remember all the messages I've received from students, young and old, the readers who tell me what a relief it is to hear stories like theirs. The ones they never get to read, the ones that paint them as human. That feeling alone is enough to satisfy me for now. I pop some gum in my mouth and try to ignore my rumbling belly as I stroll down the Kingsland Road.

Over a year later I am at a job interview with two male journalists in central London. It's a fashion editorial position, 9–5, and I've applied because I really do need a full-time job. So far, the interview has been standard: we've talked about why I wanted to get into journalism, what articles I've enjoyed working on and the awards I've won. So far, pleasant enough. It's no wonder I'm taken aback twenty minutes into the proceedings when the interviewer leans towards me.

'Do you have a Muslim agenda?' he splutters. He

looks relieved the moment it comes out of his mouth, as if he can't quite believe he managed to say it.

I chortle. 'The right-wing press are obsessed with British Muslims and it's my role to rectify myths that have an impact on a marginalized and vulnerable population,' I shoot back. I'm proud of how measured my response sounds, though I can feel my heart hammering in my ribcage.

I wonder how long he's been debating whether to ask me that – and whether he planned to long before I arrived for the interview. I roll my eyes internally.

I can barely concentrate for the rest of our conversation and at the end, the interviewer winks at me. I laugh about it on WhatsApp for hours afterwards, then stew for even longer. I can't quite shake off my anger at the fact that he clearly thought my faith meant I had an agenda – would he ask a white, male journalist writing articles on British Muslims the same question? Would he use the same accusatory tone?

I don't get the job. When I talk to a friend about it later, she says my journalism is too provocative for a fashion magazine. I tell her that I've written on more topics than British Muslims (health, food, art, social affairs) but somehow, that's the one complete strangers can't stop talking to me about.

Back to hunting through job listings, I think, deflated.

It's the end of 2017 and I'm now a multi-award-winning freelance writer and journalist. In less than two years, I've scooped three national journalism awards, including one for Young Journalist of the Year, and another, Best Feature. I'm the youngest nominee in each category. I'm proud to have carved out a career that I really love and that I get to wake up each day and write what I want to.

I think back to the summer of 2016 a lot as December looms. I wonder if I really took into account just how much the work I did put my personal safety at risk. I also wonder if my editors were aware of this. Now there's no way I would have turned up to that UKIP hustings – scouting for the closest door to escape, the rising sense of unease as Farage's name reverberated around the hall, feeling hyper-aware of being the only Muslim woman of colour in that windowless place – even if it had cost me the internship. Is it always people of colour – and women, at that – who find themselves in potentially dangerous situations as they go out on the hunt for these stories?

In 2016, when I was writing those articles on Muslim women, they often elicited the same reactions from friends and family: shock, intrigue and concern. Some labelled it a dangerous pursuit, but others were amazed by how I'd gone out to find these people and speak to them, as though there wasn't a Muslim next door or in their office that they could have struck up a conversation with. Now I see Muslims making waves around the world – in L'Oréal adverts, getting top jobs, forming art collectives.

My 2016 self would have been overjoyed, but I wonder how much has really changed. I'm still a journalist, a decision I didn't take lightly. And yes, I still receive the occasional vague threat from a troll. Anything I write on faith still comes under fire. Have we really accepted Muslim women or have we embraced the 'acceptable' face of modern Islam? The non-hijabi and the 'liberal' Muslim woman. How far have we come when we still don't really accept the multiplicities and the diversity of

Muslim women – be they conservative or those that might have a more casual relationship with faith?

I've found myself retreating to the sidelines in my journalism, dropping any provocative standpoint as if it were lava. TV and radio appearances no longer hold the same allure they once did. My safety feels too precious to risk but even so, it feels odd – even somewhat sad – that I intentionally shy away. Sometimes I'm in awe of how adventurous I was with my journalism just a few years back and that I wasn't afraid of having my name attached to my articles. There's a strange sense of satisfaction that envelops me now after spending a week away from Twitter and finding not even one notification awaiting me.

I write mostly on the 'less scary' side of journalism now: upcoming art exhibitions, photography collectives, new zine launches and profiles of women revolutionizing the food and wellness worlds. Amongst others I've written a feature on the first art exhibition to celebrate Britishness from the perspective of BAME artists for *i-D*, a profile of a food writer leading Britain's first Bengali food revolution for *VICE* 's food channel *Munchies*, and a piece on the man who set up the UK's first summer camp for trans teenagers for *Time Out London*. I still receive messages from strangers telling me how much they enjoy reading them and luckily, not once have I found a threatening email lurking in my inbox.

There's an unopened message on my Twitter and my tummy takes a tumble, a familiar paranoia emblematic of that 2016 summer.

The message is from a woman I don't know and says, simply, 'You're killing it.'

It takes more than a message from a random avatar

on Twitter to tell me what I've always felt but it feels oddly gratifying. And do you know what? I always knew it was worth it. I log out.

1 'Halal Vibrations: Exploring an X-Rated Muslim Sex Shop', *Broadly* (12 January 2016), https://broadly.vice.com/en_us/ article/9aep95/halal-vibrations-exploring-an-x-rated-muslim-sex-shop

2 '8 Things That Happen When You're Young, British And Muslim In The Weeks Following A Terror Attack', *Grazia* (5 April 2016), https://graziadaily.co.uk/life/real-life/8-things-happen-youre-young-british-muslim-weeks-following-terror-attack/

3 'British Muslim Women Talk About How It Feels to Be Constantly Spoken For', *VICE* (24 August 2016), https://www.vice.com/en_uk/article/mvkgp3/how-british-muslim-women-feel-about-constantly-being-spoken-for

4 'We Asked British Muslims What they Think of Theresa May', *VICE* (15 July 2016), https://www.vice.com/en_uk/article/8g3evx/we-asked-british-muslims-what-they-think-of-theresa-may-pm

5 'We Asked British Muslims How They Feel About a Burqa Ban', *VICE* (2 September 2016), https://www.vice.com/en_uk/article/dpkp4w/british-muslims-burqa-ban

6 'The Point: Stop policing my body', Sky News (28 September 2016), https://news.sky.com/video/the-point-stop-policing-my-body-10596483

7 'Muslim women much more likely to be unemployed than white Christian women', University of Bristol (15 April 2015), http://www.bristol.ac.uk/news/2015/april/muslim-women-and-employment.html

Shame, Shame,
It Knows Your Name

Amna Saleem

It's 8 a.m. I've yet to have breakfast, brush my teeth or get out of my pyjamas. I have, however, managed to read three direct messages, four mentions and one email from various men (it's always men) telling me who I am. To some I am a sinful woman who should know her place and to others I'm an ungrateful bitch trying to sneak sharia law into the country.

Surprise! I'm neither of these people, but I know that there are men out there who can only feel big if they can make me feel small. Except their attempts have the opposite effect. With every attempted character assassination, I grow stronger, like Popeye on spinach. You don't survive being a Muslim teenager living through 9/11 without building an efficient self-defence mechanism. Mine happens to be humour.

It's a weapon I wield at every turn, because why get angry when you can be sassy? Nothing hurts the ego of a self-important man – be he imam or racist – more than the laughter of a carefree young woman who knows what she's worth. Unless you're coming at me wearing a *dhoti*, scolding me in a Scottish-tinged Pakistani accent, then I've no fear.

I need to take this attitude, because being a Muslim feminist means being caught between radical Islamists and white supremacists (as well as your garden variety racists), which for the record isn't as fun as it sounds. While the death threats and slurs are amusing they lack creativity, which in turn results in my perpetual boredom. That's the thing: it's all entirely boring. Accusations and judgements thrown at me by society, pushy relatives or strangers on the internet are nothing new. I'm a brown Pakistani liberal Muslim who grew up in a predominately white Scottish suburb. I've literally heard it all before.

My hard-working immigrant parents were actually quite progressive, though I don't think they realized it. They had four children, two boys and two girls, but they managed to avoid raising my brothers as demigods, choosing to relegate them to this reality and thereby giving them the greatest gift of all: humility. Humility is knowing that in the grand scheme of things you are not that important. It grounds you and allows you to grow emotionally. Men who are built up by their parents to be the golden child, untouched by dishwater or manners, tend to be emotionally stunted. They lack self-awareness and respect for women. Instead, they have been taught that others should live in deference to them purely because they have a penis. This unfortunate mentality, all too common in Muslim families, allows fathers, brothers and cousins to keep the women in their family in line.

My house wasn't exactly free of gender bias, but there was no sense of superiority or entitlement ingrained into any of us from birth. As adults, my brothers aren't above setting the table, making tea for guests or crying. They weren't taught to drown in shame, whether theirs or mine. They know they aren't responsible for my 'honour' and that they don't carry the sole responsibility for familial affairs. We're all different but equal and our lives don't revolve around archaic rules that only serve to cause disharmony.

The main thing my parents encouraged was goodness. Being a good Muslim was implied because there was no distinction to them. According to my mum and dad, it's simple: if you're not a good person then the foundation of any beliefs you may hold is corrupt. As they like to say: you can fool yourself but you can't fool God. And this has been the main takeaway from my upbringing. It's what I remember every time some mosque bro tries to shame me or when a racist tries to take me down with alt-facts. Who are you fooling? I wonder, because it sure as hell isn't me.

The fact is, shame is one of the biggest drivers of toxic masculinity within South Asian culture and especially amongst Muslim men. Of course, it's usually the women whose actions provoke this dangerous emotion – often for such innocuous crimes as being seen talking to a boy, wearing an 'inappropriate' outfit, or for simply exhibiting signs of agency – but the flip side of this toxic ideal of masculinity is how it damages men themselves. This mentality nearly cost my father his life. The shame he felt for being clinically depressed was immense. He worked hard, put food on our table and was expected to sort out family disputes. A heart can only take so much, you know? And yet there was no room for my dad's suffering in our culture. According to those rules men didn't cry, they didn't ask for help and they certainly didn't admit defeat. So he was meant to suffocate his emotions. But at the expense of what? What could that do except build anger and repression? Why was that how the Muslim community wanted its men to operate?

If certain types of men in and outside my community

weren't so beholden to the ideals of masculinity, things would be better for everyone. You know what I find impressive in a Muslim man, and men in general? Being able to instil respect and not dread in his children and the people around him. Being assertive without being aggressive. Listening! Hearing the word 'no' and taking it at face value. And, no, I don't hate my community, I just know it can do better, and until we stop mollycoddling Muslim men there won't be any substantial change. There is a way to be proud of your faith without relying on misogyny and shame.

The issue of toxic masculinity and misogyny in some Muslim cultures is hardly a secret, but it's not stories like my dad's that make the news. Sadly the age of information, when fake news rules the internet, has let this shame circus run riot. For instance: the radical Islamists and the wannabe YouTube scholars who serve as pick-up artists for young Muslim men. I resent giving them any attention, which is why I won't even bother naming them or their misguided disciples, but the absurdity of their claims makes me laugh and cringe in equal measure. Among their many convoluted teachings are a series of halal sex positions that will keep men from becoming gay by accident. Yeah, you read that right: they claim that allowing a woman on top risks the manifestation of homosexuality. I don't get it either. In any case, when I have asked those adamant that these teachings feature in the Quran to show me where exactly, I suddenly get radio silence. Perhaps they lost wifi, who knows. It will remain a mystery. But there is no doubt that these people are dangerous, and that danger is twofold. They have a following – young gullible Muslim men brought up to be horrified by the shame women might bring on them – to whom they spout misogynistic nonsense, and, of course, they provide fuel for hate, giving the more racist newspapers exactly what they want: a caricature of a religion they don't understand but have set out to malign.

But where South Asian Muslim men feel too much shame, white men don't feel enough. At the extreme end we have the white supremacists. Yay! As if we didn't have enough to contend with already. On a rainy day back in August 2017, I found myself accused of being a rape apologist because I had the audacity to inform an alt-right figure – who, incidentally, is no longer allowed on Twitter – that white people didn't invent chicken tikka masala. His anger was almost palpable as he set his followers on me by twisting my words. Over chicken! Now imagine me trying to explain that to my therapist.

And it's not just the famous far-right activists. I'm constantly amazed by the speed at which racist white men, who think nothing of sending rape threats, will suddenly become radical feminists when Muslims openly try to discuss problems within our own community. For instance, when I have tried to carefully dissect difficult topics within the British Muslim community such as the Rotherham case, where sexual abuse ran rampant and unchallenged, I am pounced upon by the same racists who normally send me abuse. They suddenly applaud my 'honesty' and twist my words to fit their nefarious agenda in order to push the disingenuous message that all Muslims are culpable for the actions of one. Depending on the narrative, my words will either be used to signal that I am guilty by association or that I am a whistleblower who is finally revealing 'the truth' about my own community.

The willingness of white racists to use our community's problems as ammunition makes it incredibly hard to criticize it without feeling like a traitor. Muslim men will often insist we brush any wrongdoings, such as abuse or domestic violence, under the carpet for the sake of the community, and both the Muslim and the feminist in me is outraged when that happens. But I'm also not willing to see my community assaulted by a barrage of racism. It's all so frustrating: being a Muslim feminist too often means taking the blame for Muslim men's weakness. We are stuck between two sets of people who try to use us as pawns, then get angry when we don't oblige. I do not believe Islam and feminism clash, but due to the unavoidably fickle nature of humanity it's hard for many people to make the distinction between Islam as a religion and Muslim culture. We can continue to point out that they are two different things, but until men stop using religion as a tool of oppression we're not going to get that far.

It's a constant battle, but while it may leave Muslim feminists in limbo, it definitely does not leave us silent. I'll readily admit I'm a wee bit obnoxious and a lot scrappy, which are often words used against me: I'm loud and it forces people to take notice. I'm also super liberal on the Muslim spectrum so it's easier for me to accept certain consequences or take certain risks. But I'm aware that this isn't the case for everyone. Despite being a Muslim woman of colour I know that I am fairly privileged. I spend most of my time living in a bubble in London where everyone I know, men and women, is a progressive intersectional feminist. Admittedly it can be an echo chamber, but it makes me feel safe, especially in a time when it's not particularly easy to be Muslim. Whenever I step outside this bubble, reality is quick to hit me square in the face.

Still, I know that I can speak out on things that would get other young women into trouble. I don't risk being disowned or ostracized. While my family may find me annoying, they support me even when they don't necessarily agree with me. I have relatives who think I'm trouble and a bad influence, but I have the luxury of not giving a damn what they think. I've created a world for myself where, if my boundaries are pushed too far out of my comfort zone, the perpetrator risks losing me and not the other way round. See, the thing is, once you unlearn the internalized misogyny that is presented to you like a curse at birth, the misogynists stop having power over you. It's great; they hate it. Realizing that your self-worth is tied to more than domesticity and beauty is pretty powerful. Same goes for the racists that perpetually orbit my world: once I understood that most of their actions result from ignorance and fragile masculinity it became easier to dismiss them. I no longer feel the desire to educate them, but rather to humiliate them. It's more fun. It is not my job to appease racists, nor am I required to rise above them. This tedious high school advice is not only outdated but also dangerous, because it means that the oppressed are always required to hold a higher level of decorum than the oppressor – and that's just another mode of silencing. Needless to say, it's a notion I quickly outgrew. I do, however, believe in laughter. Laughing at them hits them where it hurts. They want your pain, your anger and your tears, but they fear your laughter. Using humour to defeat the racist trolls is an underrated strength.

Ultimately, at its creepy centre, misogyny against Muslim women is just two sides of the same grubby coin. Zealots to the left of me, racists to the right, forcing the rest of us into the middle with their nonsense.

So basically, if you're one of those men who has too much time on his hands and feels the need to try to shame me, who wants me to wear a hijab, or demands that I don't wear one, then I really don't have time for you. I'm too busy fucking shit up in the hope of making a better future for the generations that come after me. What are you doing?

A Woman of Substance

Saima Mir

My second husband gave me two things – a string of pearls, and the hard-learned lesson that life goes on. No matter what. By the time I was twenty-five, I had been married and divorced twice. I was a 'good' girl from a 'good' family. I studied hard, I was respectful to elders, I prayed five times a day, I didn't drink, and I didn't date. I liked my family and I heeded their advice. I hadn't been forced to marry, and I wasn't forced to stay. But when I made the decision to end each of my marriages, my family honour suffered. Honour is the strongest currency in South Asian families. It is the bedrock on which friendships are built and marriages are arranged. I still carry the scars of my hard-won freedom today.

Whilst Islam gives a woman the right to choose her partner and the right to leave him, Pakistani culture, the culture of my parents, does not. In some families, a daughter even expressing an interest in a potential husband is frowned upon, and in almost all families divorce is considered bad. That divorce – according to the Book of Divorce (Kitab Al-Talaq) in the *hadith* collection *Sunan Abu-Dawud* – is 'the most disliked of all permissible things in the eye of God', is often twisted to make it seem *haram*, or forbidden. It is not forbidden. It is liked the least. Out of all baked goods I like bread the least. I'm not averse to bread; I would just rather eat brioche.

I was nineteen the first time marriage was mentioned. My mother told me about a young man whose family had expressed an interest in me and promptly left the house. The realization that I was of marriageable age was clearly as difficult for her as it was surprising to me. And it really was a surprise. I was a geeky young woman who had never even shaken hands with a man, let alone had a boyfriend. I'd attended an all-girls Catholic school before opting to study science at university. My life was Malcolm X and Maya Angelou, X-Men and Spider-Man; summers were spent at my nani's house in Karachi, and winters trudging through Yorkshire snow. Bespectacled in a time before it was cool, I was short-sighted in more ways than one, young enough to believe that good things happened to good people.

My first husband was eleven years older than me. We met only once before the wedding, but spent the year leading up to the big day talking on the phone. I was in my final year at university, happily ignoring my studies and dreaming of my new life. He was a doctor – the ideal profession for a son-in-law – and the eldest of two sons, who had moved to the US from Pakistan after finishing medical school. We married on 6 September 1996, and then we flew to Mississippi where we were to set up home.

I read somewhere that if you're not embarrassed by who you were ten years ago then you're not living life deeply enough. My feelings about that time are so strong that the writing and editing of this essay makes me shaky; in fact, the first draft had me weeping. I have called my sisters after every closure of my laptop hoping to find solid ground once again, and they remind me that the woman I have become is far removed from the girl I was. Now, I feel I should have known better, but I did then what I knew then, and I was so young: twenty-one years old, and living in a pretty white doll's house of an American home, surrounded by identikit buildings. 'No children or pets' said a sign outside.

The walls of our house were pale green, the carpets beige, the wardrobes the kind you can walk into. It was the sort of open-plan house I had seen in nineties Hollywood romcoms. The living room had a single brown leather sofa and a large TV with huge free-standing speakers on either side. These speakers were my first husband's passion. He would take out a tape measure to check the distance between them, the TV and the sofa. Other than that, he was quiet, highly reserved. His mother, who lived with us, was not. Much of what happened during that time has faded, but a few things stay with me. The way she would make him sit on her lap, his embarrassment at her kisses, her coming into the bedroom whilst we slept, her odd questions about whether he used soap in the shower. For my husband, this was just his mother – one of the women he came home to in the evenings. But I spent all day at home with her. I had no money of my own, and no way of going anywhere. He would come home from work and the three of us would sit side by side on that leather sofa watching that enormous TV. When it got late, his mother would say, 'Now go straight to bed and don't talk.' When a red sock was put in with the white wash she blamed me for ruining his lab coats. When a hair scrunchie turned up in the pressure cooker she told me it was God teaching me a lesson for asking her to move her hairbrush from the kitchen work surface. I had never been faced with such behaviour. Was I losing my mind? Slowly I began to feel afraid for no reason; I lost weight – it seemed I had married a man and his mother.

I was in Mississippi on a three-month visitor visa. Immigration rules meant that if I applied for a Green Card I would be unable to return to England for at least two years. The thought of that was unbearable and my mother advised me to come home before I applied. From that point, the demise of the marriage was fast. I didn't want to live with his mother. She didn't want to live with me. It wasn't that I wanted a divorce, but I could not live in that situation. And so it ended. My husband never made any attempt to reconcile or resolve, and I never got back on the plane to the USA. My first marriage had lasted a mere three months.

At the time, divorce was very uncommon in my culture. I was lucky to have parents who trusted my judgement and didn't care what other people had to say. And people did have a lot to say. Divorce may be perfectly allowable according to Islam (in fact, Islam identifies no difference between a divorcee and a virgin – the Prophet's first wife was a divorcee), but that didn't stop the gossip. The public nature of the proclamation of *nikah* and the divorce that followed meant that everyone knew my business, and in a society that prizes virginity, my 'value' had fallen. I was sullied in a way that I would not have been if I had had a secret relationship, something which is forbidden within Islam.

The easiest way for a woman to regain her status after a divorce is to say her husband was impotent. For a culture that shies away from talking openly about sex, it is nevertheless often blamed for the end of a marriage. Female relatives who came to visit and offer condolences churned out set phrases. 'Where did he kiss you?' 'I don't believe that she's not a virgin!' 'There's clearly something wrong with him!' It would have been easy to say I was still a virgin. But that would have been a lie. The truth was simple. I had been married and I was now divorced. And though I knew there was nothing wrong with my decision, their words left me feeling dirty, as if I had been the victim of a sex crime. I remember scrubbing myself in the shower until I almost bled, trying to clean away my shame. Shame. For the first time in my life I learnt the meaning of that word.

There is a difference between guilt and shame. Guilt comes from recognizing one's own mistake. Shame is heaped upon us by others. And there is a place for shame in society. It should be heaped upon the patriarchal cultures that subjugate women. It should be felt by the women who allow it to continue, both through their silence and their actions. It should be placed upon the men who stand by and allow their mothers, their sisters, their wives and their aunts to oppress women in the name of Islam, men who benefit from their privilege. And it also belongs to the men who abandon us to its effects, simply because they are too afraid to speak up.

The shame stayed with me for many years, raising its head every now and then, stopping me in my tracks, making me feel I was no good, that I was undeserving of love. But I didn't speak of it, not until years later when I broke down in front of my sister. 'I'm ashamed, so, so ashamed,' I sobbed. The words poured out of me like water through a broken dam. I remember the shock in her voice, the heartbreak on her face. 'But you haven't done anything wrong!' she said. And somehow it had been enough. There are things that we know, things that we recognize to be true, but which must be spoken aloud by those we love to take effect. With those simple words she set me free.

Take Two

My family felt that the best way to repair the situation of my divorce was to marry me off again as soon as possible. I was reticent but they convinced me to meet someone, telling me that once I was happy I'd forget all about the past.

I was only twenty-three the second time I got married. My second husband was the opposite of the first. He was only a little older than me and was full of liveliness and excitement. He had the kind of energy that comes with youth, success and arrogance. I remember looking at his trainers the first time we met, and rejoicing. My last husband had worn Hush Puppies.

'What's stopping you saying yes?' he asked the second time we met. 'If things go wrong, I'll take a stand against my family.' He promised me that if his family interfered he would stand up for me; he promised me it would be different from my first marriage. And so I agreed to marry him. I believed him. I think back to that time and wonder why I didn't say no. Why was I so afraid? I can only say that I thought my elders knew better. I was raised as a people-pleaser; I was raised to put my own feelings aside for the sake of others. I was also raised to see the best in people, even if that meant disregarding my own instincts and intuition. I thought my family would make the right choice for me. I handed over control of my life to my parents.

But once again, I found myself living in an extended family. We lived with his mum, dad and little sister, and had frequent visits from his second sister, her husband and their two small children. There was also a third sister who lived with her extended family and who was held up by them as someone I should aspire to be like.

It soon became apparent that things were not going to be easy. The day after the wedding, we visited his parents before boarding a flight for our honeymoon. On arrival I could sense something was amiss. My father-in-law raised an eyebrow and asked me what I was wearing. I was dressed in a *ghagara*, a kind of heavily gathered skirt that skims the ground. 'A skirt,' I said. His grimace displayed his displeasure. My husband told me later that his father had an aversion to skirts and saw my wearing one as a personal affront. He had an aversion to and an opinion on many things, it would turn out.

One of the biggest issues my father-in-law had was my name. I had decided to double-barrel my surname, but when my father-in-law saw my mail, his rage knew no bounds. The strife that followed was unending, and one of my sisters-in-law was called in to give me a 'talk'. She told me that only actors double-barrelled their names. In Islam there is no ruling about changing one's name, and in fact my own grandmother never changed hers, but cowed by pressure I gave in.

I've come to believe that what followed was gaslighting: my in-laws began slowly eroding my confidence. A couple who had been at each other's throats before I arrived, his mother and father united against me. I found myself becoming a housemaid to my husband and his family. A few months in and I was cooking all the meals and cleaning the house, waiting on everyone hand and foot. The fear of arguments and their rage kept me compliant. It is difficult to explain to someone who has never experienced it how words can destroy a person. A few more months in, my eldest sister-in-law sat me down for a formal talk. She said I was neglecting my duties and needed to start doing her parents' washing and ironing. I had little say in the matter. I'd been raised to respect my elders, and this meant not arguing or answering back, not even to defend myself. Though well intentioned, this cultural teaching does us a huge disservice, and countless women find themselves slowly being worn down as their silence is taken for weakness. Islam gave women a voice; cultural interpretation took it away.

Another few months in and I was washing, ironing, cooking, cleaning and feeding everyone in the house. My duties included driving my mother-in-law to the school where she taught – an hour and a half there and back – and taking her to various mosque activities. After all this, she'd sit on the sofa whilst I served dinner, cleared plates, and then made cup after cup of tea.

My husband's role in all this was strange. I have no doubt that he loved me, that he wanted to spend time with me. We were young, we laughed at stupid things. We watched *Ally McBeal* every Thursday in our bedroom – the one time in the week we'd head upstairs before 9 p.m. (all other evenings were spent with his parents) – and we spent weekend afternoons wandering aimlessly around London only to end up in Pizza Hut. We went on beautiful holidays and he bought me lavish gifts as well as small thoughtful trinkets. I would go so far as to say he adored me. But there was another side to him, the side his parents would rile into a rage. And I would bear the brunt of it.

Once he left me sobbing on the bathroom floor because I wasn't wearing the clothes his mother had picked out for me. We were on the way to a wedding and his parents didn't approve of the blue silk *salwar kameez* and pearl choker I had on. They had a word with him just before leaving, following which he raged and spewed venom at me. I remember dropping down the wall of the bathroom, unable to breathe, my foundation washing off into my hands. His sister came to get me and I had to clean myself up and go to the wedding, where he was suddenly apologetic and loving, whispering sweetly into my ear as he held me to his side. Exhausted and empty, I accepted his apology. I had little energy for anything else.

His parents would wind him up like a clockwork toy with great regularity. It was usually just before we took a trip away, and I would spend the first couple of days 'detoxing' him. The stress on both of us was beyond breaking point. I remember sitting by a pool in Morocco, watching helplessly as he sobbed. 'They tell me I'm under my wife's thumb,' he said. 'But maybe I want to be!' I sometimes wonder what would have happened if I had been strong enough to stand up to his family, if I'd shouted and argued the way they did. But I had no desire to control him; I just wanted to live my life. The truth was his family were threatened by me, and were afraid they would lose their son to me. In their attempts to stop this happening they made my life hell.

I started working part-time to escape the stress of my in-laws. I could feel the knots in my shoulders untightening as I boarded the train that took me away from home and to the department store where I worked as a photographer. They would tighten up on the ride back. Needless to say, my mother-in-law objected to my working, picking faults in the housework, and complaining that she didn't benefit from my salary.

Their list of petty issues grew. I had not been raised properly, there was a dead fly on the steps I had failed to pick up, I had got my hair cut short without asking their permission, I'd met a friend in a coffee shop, my nani didn't visit. One day some junk mail arrived in my double-barrelled name, and my father-in-law called my husband at the investment bank where he worked. In turn, he called me, and I was shaking by the time the call ended. I could not concentrate at work. I could not relax at home. I had nowhere to go.

In the winter of 2000, just after Ramadan, I visited my parents for Eid. My husband rang and something in his tone told me all was not well. He said he wanted me to apologize to his youngest sister, the sister to whom I had given a Christian Dior compact before I left, the sister I had hugged, for whose birthday I had bought a huge bouquet, for whom I was expected to cover when she spent the night out, whom I treated as my own. But she needed an apology. She was upset about the way I had spoken to her in front of my cousin. I refused, telling him it was none of his business. He shouted. I refused again. Maybe it was because I was home safe with my parents, or maybe I had taken as much as I could bear. Whatever it was, I was done.

What remained of the marriage crumbled quickly. I watched my kind, warm father silently listen to the venom my father-in-law poured down the phone. It is something I can never forgive, the pain that was caused by them to my family. Islam states that daughters are blessings, that the man who treats his daughters kindly and educates them will be with the Prophet in heaven. But culture dictates that the families of women bear their pain stoically. It is their fate. It is utter bullshit.

I did try to reconcile with my husband, but something in me knew he would never leave his parents' house. I remember arriving at his office in Liverpool Street, having travelled from Bradford Interchange alone to have this conversation. It was my last hope; I needed to look into his eyes and hear what he had to say. I called him from the station and asked him to come and meet me. He refused, his voice hard, his tone cold. After much convincing he came to see me. 'Go home,' he said. That was all he kept saying. He meant to his home in Essex. I tried to take his arm and he shook me off. What a fool I was, to allow a man such power over me, to almost beg for a relationship that should never have happened. Broken and devoid of hope, I sat down on a bench in the station, weeping as I called my grand-mother. I remember looking up to see a billboard advertising a Hannibal Lecter movie . . . 'Ever felt like a piece of meat?' it read. And I did.

And so I applied for *khula*, the Islamic form of divorce that is granted when a woman wishes to leave her husband. Seated in a small room in the mosque, my parents beside me, and my husband and his father in front, I asked for a divorce. 'But I don't want to give it,' my husband said to the *qadi*. There is a misconception that Islam does not allow a woman the right to divorce her husband. This lie is spread and made powerful by the halting of the education of girls and women by men, by cultural stigma, and by the *mullahs* who want to maintain power. But a woman who can read the Quran soon learns that her subjugation and oppression is a man-made construct, very much against the law of Allah and his prophet. She learns that Islam gives her the right to choose her own spouse, and the right to leave a man she does not like. He must release her with kindness and return to her what is hers. Schooled in Islamic *sunnah*, and raised by a grandmother with a deep understanding of the Quran, I was an educated woman. I knew my place. And it was not as the workhorse of an abusive household.

'I don't need your permission,' I said coldly. It was the first time I had felt such resolve.

'She's right,' the *qadi* said. 'She doesn't need your permission.'

'But I don't want to give it!' My husband's voice was rising, his discomfort writ large across his face.

The *qadi* nodded at me and confirmed that he could dissolve the marriage immediately. 'All you have to say is that you don't want to be married to this man.'

'I don't want to have anything more to do with these people,' I said, looking into my father-in-law's eyes. A stunned expression spread across his face. He had assumed me to be weak, that a woman who was already divorced once would be oppressed and beaten into submission, that I would be so cowed by the reaction of the culture that I would do anything to avoid the shame again. They had taken my kindness for weakness. But I knew what it meant to be happy, and I knew I deserved better than what they offered.

The papers were signed and I watched as my now ex-husband, dejected and small, turned to his father, his face pained, and said, 'But you said it wouldn't happen today.'

The actual granting of my divorce was as simple as that, because Islam makes it that easy. It was culture and its contradictions that made my life complicated.

My nani taught me that Islam is simple. 'It is about two things,' she said, 'loving God and loving his people.' And in this fight to be good Muslims, that is the bedrock on which we should build our faith. The discussions around women, who we marry, what we eat, drink, wear, are moot if, at the end of the day, they are imposed upon us by anyone other than our own conscience. Islam connects each person with their maker directly. He is closer to us than our jugular vein. So, why then do people think they can and should come between him and us?

My second husband and I were young. He listened to his parents and fell foul of his own temper and his family's manipulation. We all make mistakes.

We spoke a few years ago, and I asked him how he could have been so cold. 'I'm sorry if that's how it came across,' he said. 'It wasn't like that.' We spoke for only a few minutes, but in that time he said the things I had wanted him to understand all those years ago. 'Times have changed and our women have changed with them, but our men have yet to catch up.'

I often hear about the negative effects of divorce. No one tells you about the good. Through the heartbreak, the loss, the failure, is a better place. A place of greater understanding. A place of broken egos and emotional growth. We, two people who had once loved each other, became better people by leaving each other. Whispered words, raucous laughter, the sharing of intimate secrets – these are hard enough to leave behind without the judgement of society adding to it. But it does. And patriarchy pushes it along.

Take Three

My husband jokes that I was mistrustful of him when we met. He's wrong. I may not have trusted him. But I didn't distrust him either. I was open and aware.

Culture had condemned me despite my having done

everything according to the laws of Islam, so I had decided to reject culture's rules.

After my second divorce my father told my mother: 'You will never stop my daughters doing what they want again.' Having raised us as equals with our brother, he had had enough of his girls being maligned. After this, we stopped pandering to the community. Outwardly, I merged my eastern and western wardrobes, mixing *kurtas* with jeans and shawls. Inwardly, I stopped giving a damn about gossip. The worst had happened. I was the talk of the town and there was nothing more to lose.

With my personal life dead, my professional life flourished. I was twenty-seven when I landed a traineeship at my local paper thanks to a brilliant features editor who put up with my pestering emails. I had never set foot in a newsroom and once I did, I knew I was home. The paper gave me a job and sent me to journalism school. My pleasures were simple – a trip to Blockbuster and a pizza on a Sunday night – but they were bought with my money and without compromise.

Just a few years later I was working for the BBC. My father was impossibly proud, recording every news item I was in and boring visitors half to death. When I moved out and into my own place, the mosque tongues wagged that I'd fallen out with my folks. They didn't know it was my father who had found the cottage in the heart of Bradford, made the viewing appointment, and arranged for me to see a mortgage broker. My father understood the importance of freedom.

I'd come home from weddings to my cottage and climb into my big comfy double bed alone. I'd sleep in, eat croissants in bed with mugs of hot tea as I read the Sunday papers, all the while knowing that old Asian aunts pitied my single life. I'd imagine them in their messy houses with their irritating husbands and over-bearing mothers-in-law whispering about the life I had brought upon myself. My mother, of course, was still concerned. What decent man would marry me, especially now I was on TV? Nice Pakistani girls did not appear on screen. But I had made a promise: to live life on my own terms. I'd make mistakes but they'd be my mistakes. I had no intention of getting married again. My mother had other ideas.

It was a Saturday when my sister texted me to tell me Mum had given yet another guy my number. 'Don't shoot the messenger,' her text read. Several dead messengers were already strewn across the paths to my house and work, but this time, I put down my gun. I took a deep breath and waited. 'It will be an interesting two weeks after which he'll turn out to be an arsehole, and I'll cry for a bit, and then it will be over,' I told her.

He texted on the Sunday night. I responded with a long list of my availability. He called and we talked. He sounded normal, but he also wasn't the guy Mum had given my number to. It turned out he had been given my number six months earlier by one of my aunts, but shortly afterwards his father had passed away. It was whilst going for a walk one cold October day that he'd found the little piece of paper in a coat he hadn't worn since.

We gave each other the relationship résumé. 'Serves me right for putting all my eggs in one bastard,' I said. He laughed loudly and unapologetically. Something clicked in my head and I relaxed. Two weeks later he came to meet me in Leeds. We ate lunch, walked around, talked. He bought me three books – *The Reluctant Fundamentalist*, *What the Dog Saw* by Malcolm Gladwell, and a book of love poems. I felt heard. When it was time for him to leave, we walked to the station so he could catch his train. *Well, that was pleasant enough*, I thought.

Over the following months, we continued talking every night and boarding trains back and forth between London and Bradford. And after much hard work on his part, I eventually agreed to marry him. I could see in him the life I wanted to build. And something told me that if I said no, I would regret it. I had learnt that, contrary to cultural expectations, good relationships are good from the start and not something to be achieved through effort.

My husband isn't religious, but he proved how much he wanted to marry me by visiting the mosque every day for two weeks to get our *nikah* papers signed. But the experience put him off future visits. 'Saima Mir, BBC?' the imam said, on hearing who his intended was. 'Are you sure you want to marry her?' And there it was. Despite my husband's lack of belief, the fact he had no connection to the mosque, and his having married (and then divorced) someone of another sect, patriarchal culture considered *him* too good to marry *me*. My husband was furious. By mixing patriarchal culture with religion, the imam turned a good man off Islam.

Finale

More than eight years on and I can tell you I made a wise choice. I am still married to a good and kind man. I am now the mother of two young boys, and I feel the privilege and pressure of raising them as good Muslim men.

At some point they will take down this book from the shelf and read my story. I hope that by then they will have a deep understanding of my faith. They will know that Islam gives a woman the right to choose her partner and to leave him with only the reason that she doesn't like him. Where a man needs to state his desire to divorce his wife on three separate occasions, a woman need only make the request once.

Islam sees women as practical in matters of divorce; we think deeply before leaving a man. Men can be hot-headed. Women, less so. Yet, culture punishes a woman who leaves. She is devalued because she has had sexual relations. She is ungrateful and therefore sinful for wanting contentment, happiness, and a life free of abuse.

For too long Islam has been interpreted through the eyes of men. If, as we are taught, God loves his people many times more than a mother, can a man judge what that love feels like, and how much space for growth and bad judgement that encompasses?

I will forever be the woman who left two husbands. And although writing this essay has been akin to standing naked in a roomful of mirrors, it has been cathartic, and as I type the last few words, I find I am proud of my fight. I dared to break free of patriarchy. I refused to conform. I also refused to give up my religion, and Islam backed me up all the way.

Despite the naysayers and judges, I have found all the simple things I wanted at the start: the love of a good man, a happy home and healthy children. Surely, this should be every woman's right.

I am an emancipated Muslim woman. There is no contradiction in this.

A Gender Denied: Islam, Sex and the Struggle to Get Some

Salma El-Wardany

I lose my virginity in a way that surprises even me. It is unassuming. Comes without dilemma and as naturally as the break of dawn. It is easy. Painless. Safe. It takes place in a house with parents, albeit not my own, but the comforting presence of adulthood brings a subconscious assurance to the proceedings.

I lose my virginity in love. The desperately naive sort that is *first* love: a time when you're yet to taste the bitterness the world will later offer you.

All of this to say that, as an Egyptian Muslim girl, losing my virginity outside wedlock, to a white, Yorkshire boy who was unsure whether God even existed, was one of the sweetest moments of my life. Perhaps even one of the purest. Nothing lay between us but blind faith and abundant hope. An absolute conviction that we held love in our palms, and somewhere I knew God must be behind this. How else could such a love exist? It remains one of the few moments in my life that God and I were in perfect agreement with one another. An understanding existed between us and everything around me flowed in harmony. As if the world had been painted just for me that day.

My experience, however, was not the norm. When I finally sailed down from the cloud of new awareness and womanhood I had ascended to, my conversations with Muslim girlfriends told me that my blithe happiness was a far cry from their own emotions and I realized something was wrong. 'Did you feel guilty?' was the first question asked, followed by, 'did you pray after?' The not-so-subtle message was that a sin had been committed and now was the time for redemption.

In truth, I knew I had crossed a line. I, like my friends, had been raised on the collective teachings of an Islamic community that argued sex only happened within the parameters of marriage, and any kind of relationship with boys was ultimately *haram*. I was not only raised on those teachings, but I also believed and bought into them, adamant that I would lose my virginity on my wedding night with my husband. It's hard not to adopt this narrative when the lessons of chastity are so intricately woven, both consciously and subconsciously, throughout the subtle workings of Islamic spaces. We learn very early on that lines are never blurred, and an impenetrable barrier exists between men and women. Consider segregation in mosques: the genders split to enter through different doors, then worship in different rooms. For a young Muslim, it is the first indication that liaising with the opposite sex is not acceptable, a message that is then reinforced by the cultural segregation of social spaces. Even the interactions between family and friends send a message: men hug men and women kiss women, but everyone is careful never to touch anyone outside their own gender, no matter how much 'like family' they are. In short, we have grown up in environments that have consistently told us that men and women don't mix, a constant spotlight on the division between the two. Add in the narrative that sex is *haram* – and of course anything *haram* is punishable by hellfire – and it's easy to understand why so many women discuss sex, shame and guilt in the same sentence. They have become so tangled with one another that they're now part of a single conversation. And the reason they have become part of the same conversation is that you cannot talk about sex in Islam without also encountering culture and the patriarchy.

Nothing exists in isolation and Islam's theological rulings on sex are no exception, prone to cultural distortions that lead to a skewed perception of sexuality, especially female sexuality. If you delve into the *hadith* and recommendations from scholars, or if you're brave enough to watch the YouTube videos of prominent sheiks doling out advice (mostly for the benefit of men), you'll find things like the commonly quoted *hadith* from the Book of Marriage in the collection *Sahih Al-Bukhari*: 'if a man calls his wife to his bed and she refuses, and he spends the night angry with her, the angels will curse her until morning.' You can even find arguments in favour of female circumcision. One regurgitates ideas taken from a debate that was held in 1950s Cairo, in which a protagonist argued that if a woman experiences sexual pleasure, it might exhaust a man to the point of death.[1]

These are not obscure references, but commonly repeated interpretations quoted out of context and out of time, and yet they are still regularly called on to elicit the desired behaviours from women. The mindset that a woman might do the unthinkable and refuse a man, or that she could even kill a man through the shameful use of her sexuality, means that men believe women need to be controlled, and this theory is conveniently backed up by supposed theology, providing a safety blanket for a wider community that is polluted by chauvinism and fragile male pride. The devastating truth is that it works. Women are given information that is heavily informed by a patriarchal scholarship, and they believe it, internalize it, and begin to live their life within its narrow confines – because after all, who wants to be cursed by angels all night? It's also important to note that information regarding sex in Islam is not readily available, and when we don't even possess the spaces to talk about it, it becomes impossible to safeguard women and facilitate healthy conversations.

For the purpose of this essay I spoke to over two hundred Muslim women across the globe, and there wasn't a single one who had a place within her community to talk about sex and Islam. A few were lucky to come from families in which mothers were willing to have open and non-judgemental conversations about sex, but they were rare exceptions. The two things that most of the women I spoke to knew about sex were that anal sex and sex during menstruation are forbidden. That, it seems, is the extent of knowledge and information we are passing on to women as they prepare for their first sexual encounters. Muslim women are only taught what is wrong, never what is allowed, and they are never encouraged or shown the ways in which two people can, and should, enjoy one another. The stories I've heard from Muslim women all have a common thread of shame running through them, and sometimes the messaging is so strong that even on their wedding nights with their Muslim husbands, these women have been unable to enjoy sex because somewhere in their subconscious remains the residue of a fire and brimstone upbringing and the idea that, even though they've been married with the blessing and joy of their families behind them, they are doing something wrong. If you tell someone something for long enough, they will eventually believe it, and unlearning is a difficult process. I've heard stories of marriages breaking down because of women unable to enjoy or accept a sexual relationship, or even years of painful sex because of the tension created by fear and guilt. Then, of course, there are the women who were never spoken to about sex at all, their chastity and virginity glorified until their wedding nights, when they were suddenly expected to perform with the sexual prowess of an accomplished lover.

It is also important to recognize the huge difference between the biological act of sex and the gratification two people can derive from one another. The absence of female pleasure from conversations about sex is keenly felt within Muslim communities, but not limited to them. No one is lucky enough to escape the patriarchy, and as such the mentality that female bodies are there to give pleasure as opposed to receive it is a long-standing one. Combine this with the cultural shame we've imposed on women, and do it all in the name of Islam, and you're in danger of creating swathes of frustrated women, fearful of sex, too ashamed to talk about it, and unable to access pleasure.

There are, and always will be, exceptions to the rule. In various corners of the world you will find groups of Muslim women sitting together joking about the wedding night, or a mother somewhere giving her daughter condoms, hopeful that whatever her daughter is going to do, she will do it in safety. In Egypt, value is placed on the youth and beauty of women, and while sex is never spoken about directly, there is a rich web of traditions that allude to and celebrate it. For example, the week before a woman is married, when she does her *halawa* for the first time, information is laughingly passed between women, and these gatherings take on a voluptuousness as older women offer advice, smiles and jokes, and the community prepares the bride for her wedding night and the start of the next chapter in her life.

Yet still, behind the jokes and the prenuptial traditions there is a barrier to basic education and pleasure. The conversations that do see the light of day are normally within the context of wedding nights and halal encounters, and even then it can be argued that they centre on the act of a man coming to your bed and taking his pleasure, as opposed to the woman receiving an equal sum of pleasure. Without the right information to hand, Muslim women are introduced to sex in ways that can be damaging, painful, unsafe and traumatic. In my own family, stories have been passed down from the days in the villages in Egypt when the new husband would enter the bedroom with his mother and penetrate his wife, and once the hymen was broken, the mother-in-law would come out with blood on a handkerchief as evidence of her new daughter's virtue. These tales seem medieval and brutal to the modern listener, but nevertheless the lingering memories of these cultural practices send inhibiting messages about virginity and chastity to subsequent generations.

Growing up in England, there wasn't a hint of female blood apparent in our Islamic community, which is no surprise as you could barely mention your menstrual cycle without being hushed by the women and sending the men into instant panic. I very much doubt they'd have been able to stomach a woman waving a deflowered virgin's blood about the local mosque. However, the fragmented Muslim diaspora is in no way immune to the cultural hang-ups of their origin countries. In fact, often Muslim communities in the West are more resistant to change or modernization, because they already exist in worlds that would have them change everything. Resisting change is a defence mechanism, and so by proxy, they cling on to waning mentalities about sex and a stubborn refusal to adapt. This stubbornness then manifests in the way they raise their children, pouring their own longing for their home country into the small humans in their charge, the idea being that perhaps if they instil enough of 'back home', and enough of Islam into their sons and daughters, they might be safe from the evil temptations of western countries. The reality was that instead of planting love of home in us they planted outdated rules that grew crops of silence, and so the secrets began to blossom from our lips.

When rules tighten and teachings become iron-fisted, you begin to hide what you're doing, and now we have a new generation of Muslim women growing up in western countries with no safe spaces to have conversations about sex, turning to the internet and the cruel lessons of pornography. My first introduction to sex was via Google and watching porn, which – as we all know – is rarely about female empowerment or pleasure and more often about female submission. I remember using the handle of a toothbrush to poke around to see what would happen – would it make me moan like the women in those videos? Needless to say, it did not, and I found the entire experience more confusing than anything else. My sexual education was a blur of videos, misinformation, miscellaneous objects, hidden fumbles with boys and finally a boyfriend who I loved, but who I had to keep hidden for over a year of our three-year relationship.

I'm thirty years old now, unmarried and single. I've loved and been loved but never found the right person to marry and make a life with. If the Islamic community had it their way, I would still not have experienced pleasure, or a loving relationship, because I've yet to find a husband. Unlike me, many Muslim women choose to operate within the constraints of their culture, but regardless of whether we decide to deviate from or play by the rules, we have to get better at creating open environments for women to have the conversations they have previously been denied. This might look like weekly classes, a designated elder to speak to, a way to submit anonymous questions, peer education or monthly gatherings. It might be different for each community and happen in different ways, but there definitely needs to be a community commitment to educating girls and women. The same needs to happen for boys and men, of course, as they are just as badly affected by this misinformation and by the sexual entitlement promoted amongst men in Muslim communities. Muslim men can often be routine and systematic in their approach to sex, the years of privilege manifesting between the sheets as they take their pleasure without considering female satisfaction. We need spaces for them to unlearn inherent misogyny and begin a sexual education that emphasises the participation of two people in sex, not just one.

The way our communities are dictatorial about marriage is also problematic. I fell deeply in love with a boy outside Islam and if I could have, I would have married him at the time. However, like other Muslim girls, I had been raised with the commonly accepted interpretation of the Quran that states a Muslim man can marry a non-Muslim woman, but a Muslim woman cannot marry a non-Muslim man. I was in an impossible situation, hiding my relationship, unable to talk to the adults I knew about it, and feeling guilty in the knowledge that the boy I loved wasn't welcome in the spaces I existed in – whether that was at Eid prayers, amongst my Pakistani family or visiting my Egyptian relatives overseas. This man was a foreigner and not somebody I, as a 'good Muslim girl', should ever be with. Those narratives are hopelessly difficult to resist, and we are all affected by the habits, traditions and beliefs of our communities; I'm no exception to those rules. I often look back and wonder whether, if my community had opened their arms to him, if we'd known that sometime soon we could be married, if there were people I could talk to about marrying outside the religion, things would have been different for me. I wonder if I might have waited to have sex with him, safe in the knowledge that we had all the time in the world. I wonder if we'd be married now, surrounded by a tribe of children. I wonder if I would have been protected from the heartbreak and pain that came as a result of trying to please a community that demanded I live by their rules only.

I'm not a scholar of Quranic verses, Arabic etymology or the *hadith* of the Prophet (peace and blessings be upon him), all of which are needed to fully understand the nuances of sex in Islam and what is theologically permitted. However, I do know certain things to be absolutely true. The first is that the current scholarship and material on Islam is not fit for purpose within the context of our modern lives. This is not to argue that we need an entirely liberal re-reading of the Quran; but we do need one that is translated by a female scholar, without the trappings of male chauvinism stamped on it. We need to understand the ways in which men and women are actually living today, as opposed to how we wish they were living, and learn how to navigate modernity and Islam together, especially when it comes to conversations around sex and sexuality. People are having it, have been having it, will keep having it, regardless of whether or not you tell them it's a sin. Fire and brimstone theology has rarely been conducive to spirituality and faith, and is arguably detrimental to an inclusive and functional society. It serves only to oppress, alienate and traumatize, all things that will eventually be the map people use to leave Islam rather than to accept its beauty into their lives in ways that fit. Young Muslims might not be living Islam in the ways their parents had hoped, but they are still living it, and the louder the ringing of the word sin reverberates through them, the harder it gets to live in Islamic communities. People want to remove 'sinners' from the religion because it's the easiest way to deal with them, but perhaps it is time for quiet mouths and open arms instead of scarlet letters and pointed fingers.

Secondly, the way our communities are structured desperately needs to change, starting with addressing the cultural obsession with segregation that is forced onto every Islamic gathering. When I was seventeen years old, I was standing in the corridor of my local mosque, the *masjid* I had been a part of since I was five years old, when I was told off for talking to my brother. When I replied furiously that we were related, I was told that 'the rest of the mosque didn't know that' and therefore I couldn't speak to him. On another occasion my father told me not to walk too closely to my (male) best friend. When I reminded him my friend was gay, I was told once more that other people didn't know that, and I shouldn't be walking too closely to a boy anyway. A girl being seen in public with a boy is too damaging to her reputation and the consequences of a tarnished reputation naturally too dire, and so distance must always be enforced. My adolescence is full of experiences like this: messages that consistently reinforced segregation, threatened damnation, and taught me that if I kept far away enough from boys and men, I would be fine.

Another side effect of this segregation is that the Muslim friends we make end up being of our own gender, and when the time comes to pick a suitable partner and marry ('suitable' meaning Muslim), we don't know any Muslim men. Two of my nearest and dearest friends are Muslim women I grew up with, and between us we're not in contact with a single boy from our community. We weren't allowed to hang out with them, not even under the watchful eyes of our community, yet when we got older we were suddenly expected to marry them. It's little wonder we fell for the non-Muslim men outside our religious spaces, only to be told we could never be with them, while not being afforded any other options. It's a Catch-22 that leaves entire generations of Muslim women in impossible situations. To segregate so completely is an insult to both genders. We're assuming that men are so lacking in control around women that they must be cordoned off, and we're dehumanizing women, creating caricatures of sexual temptation that must be kept hidden, extolling chastity as a means of control. Islam has never been about avoiding the opposite gender and creating barriers, but instead about mutual respect and collaboration, and those things cannot happen when women are being stuffed into corners and hidden from sight.

Thirdly, and most importantly, we must start having conversations about female pleasure. Both sexes are in desperate need of an entirely new education system so that Muslim men can unlearn the oppressive habits they've picked up from a world designed only to please them, and so that women can unlearn the silence that has been rooted in them for so many years. As we fight for gender parity we cannot underestimate the power of pleasure within this struggle. Muslim communities must start accepting women as sexual creatures who have as much right to access information, knowledge, desire and gratification as their male counterparts. We need to view women in a new light, away from the shadows of shame, guilt and age-old stereotypes that have been inflicted upon them. We need to celebrate them for the incredible things their bodies can do, revere the ways in which they give life, and attribute an appropriate level of respect for their sexual wants and needs. Notions of female sexuality have so long been out of women's hands that we are either sexually oppressed or hyper-sexualized, and those two narratives leave us torn between unrealistic dichotomies we can never live up to. The silence must be pulled by the roots and cast aside as something no longer beneficial to our growth, and we must be the ones to start that process. Whether it's vocalizing our desires to husbands and lovers, or creating circles of women who discuss and share their experiences, we must learn to do what we haven't done, what we have been trained not to do: to say out loud the things we want.

In the absence of information it is easy to think you're getting 'screwed over', and in the case of Muslim women they quite literally are. With the doors to conversation, knowledge and information shut, sex happens *to* them, not with or for them, and they're unable to enter into a world of pleasure and empowerment that's free from guilt and shame. The silence we have blanketed over our cultural communities in the name of religion has done a huge disservice to our women and girls. I often wonder if, had I not swallowed silence, I might not have found myself in an abusive relationship, the effects of which I am still struggling with years and years later. Silence is *not* golden and it hasn't been for some time now. We have to start talking so that we can learn, share, grow and change. There are conversations waiting to be had on how we nurture women and girls on a community level, while also creating societies that support gender-neutral spaces and allow marriage and interaction to happen freely. The female companions of the Prophet Mohammed (pbuh) would marry multiple times because they wanted to conduct sexual relations within the boundaries of Islam, and it's time to start talking about how we make that possible again. It's also worth remembering that celibacy is not recommended as a path in Islam and not recommended as a life choice, and we should be telling our young people that, encouraging them to have meaningful relationships.

When sexual satisfaction is hard to access and silence thrown over an entire group of people, women will find their own solutions outside what is culturally acceptable. It has been true for me, and for the Muslim women around me, and it will be true for thousands of others. I hope the conversations we're having within the pages of this book, and the stories we're sharing, encourage and support the women who have struggled to start, or have wanted to have, these discussions. I pray they give women and girls the courage to spit out the silence between their teeth and reject the uncomfortable dichotomies our Muslim and western communities have forced us into. I hope our collective shout can blur the solid line that exists between culture, family and religion on one side, and emotion, self-expression and sexuality on the other.

I hope we banish the word *haram* from our dialogue and can be a little kinder to one another, a little softer and a little more understanding. I hope our discussions have the power to lift our arms higher and wider, to welcome all manner of Muslims into our fold, whether they're out getting laid every night or not. I so want us to be able to nurture a little more. Love a lot more. Tell our stories every day. Share our sexual experiences in rays of sunlight as opposed to whispering them in dark corners. I want us to stand up and into our power as women and glory over the incredible things our bodies can do. I want us to welcome pleasure into our skin and realize that religion is not just for the few, but for the many, and that it also comes in many forms. The fluctuations and harmonies of our physicality do not bar us entry to spirituality and faith, but rather remind us of our relationship with the divine.

---

1   Abu Bakr Abdu'r Razzaq, *Circumcision in Islam* (London, 2010)

How Not to Get Married

(or why an unregistered nikah is no protection for a woman)

Aina Khan OBE

All faiths should be equal in the eyes of the law. That is something I believe is fundamental to a modern society. As a Muslim woman and a lawyer who for over twenty-five years has been committed to bridging the gap in knowledge between Islamic and secular law, I have spent my life fighting for this principle. So it is hard to accept that in twenty-first-century Britain, depending on the faith you follow, you have a high chance of being left with no legal rights after your marriage.

The UK's Marriage Act 1949 is nearly seventy years old and has never been updated. It still states that only Church of England, Jewish and Quaker marriages must be legally registered. Followers of every other faith can volunteer to register their marriage. But if they do not take steps to protect their legal rights, that marriage will not be recognized by law. To put this in perspective, as of 2017 there were around 12,934 Quakers in the UK,[1] whereas there were 2.7 million Muslims in the 2011 Census and growing.[2] Marriage law has never kept pace with immigration.

In the UK we do not have any legal rights for cohabitees (those who live together without marriage) nor is this likely for many years to come, because of the special legal status given to marriage. But without a legally recognized marriage, people become caught in a 'double whammy': under the impression that their marriage protects them, but in fact living in a union that provides no legal protection. In an English court, judges call unregistered religious marriages 'non-marriages'.

There are usually two steps to getting legally married in England and Wales. Firstly you have to give notice at your local register office (unless you are getting married in an Anglican church, in which case the officials performing the ceremony must register the marriage), and then have a religious ceremony or civil ceremony at least twenty-eight days after giving notice. A religious wedding can take place in a church or other registered religious building (including mosques that are registered to perform marriages and then file certificates at the local register office).[3]

An overseas marriage will be recognized in the UK: so long as you follow the correct process according to local law, you will not have to register it again in the UK. It is all very confusing, and because the government has always shown a laissez-faire attitude to different religions, the scene has been set for chaos. Two British sisters might each get married and believe their situations to be identical. But if one has travelled abroad for her *nikah* ceremony whilst the other has had the same *nikah* ceremony in the UK, but hasn't then gone on to legally register her marriage, that sister has a 'non-marriage': if her relationship breaks down she could be left homeless overnight as she is – in the eyes of the court – nothing more than a girlfriend.

This simply should not happen. In January 2014, I launched a campaign called Register Our Marriage (ROM).[4] I felt strongly about this lack of justice, and I wanted to challenge an out-of-date law and raise national awareness. ROM was born from my hunch that trouble was brewing. No one had data on the number of unregistered marriages that were taking place in the UK. I could not wait till someone, somewhere, did the research whilst women and children were suffering hourly, daily. So, despite objections that I had no statistics, I started spreading awareness based on my own observations and experience. I had seen a huge rise in the past five years in young Muslims not registering their marriages – in my estimation around 80 per cent of under-thirties – while most mosques seemed to have stopped registering marriages.

Imams confirm that the situation has shocked them. An example was given recently by Dr Musharraf Hussain of the Karimia Institute at a symposium we spoke at together, at the University of Oxford on 25 June 2018: 'As an imam, I perform dozens of marriages a year. I believe *nikahs* should be registered, so in 2012 I applied for my mosque to be authorized to perform legal marriages. The registrar's office recently asked me to file at least seven marriage certificates so I could continue my licence. But in the last five years, because of resistance from my congregation, I have hardly registered one marriage a year. The law needs to change to require *nikahs* to be registered.'

Because women in such unregistered marriages cannot get a legal divorce, if the husband refuses to give an Islamic divorce, they are referred to as 'chained women'. When a man refuses to give a *talaq* divorce, a wife can get a *khula* divorce – but this is often to her detriment.

Firstly, because it is not 'fault-based', she has to give up the *mahr* financial settlement set out in her Islamic marriage contract. If she does not want to give up the *mahr* she should instead obtain a *tafreeq* (a judge's divorce given on the basis of the husband's fault). However, this is rarely talked about and nowadays a woman needs to specifically ask for it.

Secondly, she has to apply to a sharia council (or in an Islamic country, an Islamic judge called a *qadi*), often facing long delays, fees, and being forced to reconcile or accept a poorer financial settlement or arrangements for children.

A wife can have a *tafweed* (right to divorce) in her marriage contract, but this is also a rarity. Women are unaware of the right, or are persuaded not to have this right – or in the majority of cases, it is simply struck out of the pro forma *nikah* marriage contract without asking them. Without the right to *tafweed*, a woman has to resort to a sharia council for a divorce. An example of a sharia council is the Muslim Law (Sharia) Council UK based in London, set up by the late Dr Zaki Badawi, a highly respected British Egyptian scholar.[5] As no one has an accurate idea of how many Muslim marriages and divorces are taking place, we can only draw on small sample studies. The latest academic research, by Cardiff University in 2011, showed that half of women applying to sharia councils for Islamic divorce were in unregistered marriages.[6]

Since then, the situation had become dire. Mosques around the country had spoken to me because of my national ROM road shows. Imams told me repeatedly that they were under pressure from their congregation not to register marriages as it would lead to women having legal rights. I cannot express how depressing it was hearing my fears confirmed. We had gone backwards twenty years. In the 1990s and earlier, registration was the norm and women would refuse proposals if the man or his family suggested not registering. People accepted that in Islam, wives and children have legal rights and this is non-negotiable. But growing unhindered in the UK was a cultural malaise born of deeply problematic patriarchal and misogynistic views of marriage as a means of control – the exact opposite of what Islam teaches.

Unhappily, instead of helping to resolve the issue, most mosques were increasingly choosing not to be registered to perform marriages. Most imams had no idea of the legal impact on couples. Some imams were resistant to becoming registered to perform legal marriages because of their fear of being forced to officiate same-sex marriages (I told them there is an exemption under the law for faith-based objections to this and they were reassured). Many simply wanted to avoid the administration and paperwork. I even spoke to a few who, most worryingly of all, no longer even prepared their own mosque's *nikah* certificate, which would at least confirm the marriage was binding in Islam. They were simply carrying out oral *nikahs* because of pressure from the community and their own desire not to get involved in marital disputes. But these *nikahs* were easily denied when the marriages broke down or after the husband's death.

But why are young Muslims less and less inclined to register their marriages? I have come to conclude these are the main reasons:

Firstly, it is worth remembering wider trends in society. The popularity of marriage is at an all-time low across the UK.[7] That is, to a degree, understandable when you consider people's fears that it could all go wrong. Some individuals want to be able to walk away without any fallout, and they fear commitment. They want to have the big party in front of their family and community, but do not want to worry about what is going to happen if the relationship breaks down. The perceived headache of a divorce, the cost of going to court, and ongoing maintenance are all certainly driving factors in this trend towards marriages not being registered. Then consider this wider societal trend from a Muslim point of view. Like thousands of other young couples, many Muslims think, 'We'll commit one day, but we are not ready yet.' The key difference is that Muslims cannot live together or have a sexual relationship without marriage. An unregistered religious marriage allows them the chance for perceived 'halal dating': being with someone without a legal commitment but with a religious and community stamp of approval.

Complacency is commonplace too. It is all too easy to have a *nikah* marriage in the UK, plan to register it ('we'll get around to it soon'), then for things to go wrong before registration takes place. In addition, there is the undeniable fact that the law is poorly communicated and people are simply ignorant about their legal position. Many assume that even if their marriage is not legally registered, living together gives them legal rights, but in the UK it does not. That confusion is understandable when you remember that getting married in a Muslim country means you have to register it, since you need a marriage certificate to make an ID card, and sometimes even to get a hotel room (when you might be asked to prove you are married). As an overseas *nikah* marriage is accepted in the UK as a legally binding marriage, people assume that having a UK *nikah* marriage must also be legally binding.

Also of great importance are cultural factors. A woman may have been brought up to believe that all that matters is the Islamic marriage and that she must have faith that her spouse will be God-fearing and will not take advantage of her. This behaviour is very hard to change: if her family do not and have never registered marriages, she is unlikely to. On the other side of the coin, where the breakdown of a legally registered marriage would grant financial rights to both parties, many want to keep wealth in the family; an unregistered marriage will guarantee that. We cannot overlook the fact that unregistered marriages have actively encouraged polygamy. There is nothing to stop a Muslim man taking multiple wives, so long as his marriages are not legally registered and he does not commit bigamy. Some Muslim women have publicly said they want to be second or third wives because they want a 'part-time' husband, even if the first wife is being deceived. There are now both online sites and large-scale formal events in the UK offering meetings for this purpose.*

A great many people think the *nikah* marriage is legal because that is what they are told by their community. When they find out it is not, often in front of a solicitor, it comes as a horrendous shock. To trust someone and believe that your marriage is legal, only to find that your spouse planned all along not to give you rights – that betrayal is hugely destructive. The unpleasant truth is that unofficial marriages such as these can lead to human rights abuses – and it is usually women and children who

---

* Two examples include https://www.secondwife.com and this article in the *New Statesman* https://www.newstatesman.com/lifestyle/religion/2013/04/what-kind-woman-willing-share-her-husband

are left vulnerable. Even when the union has been a happy one, the widow of an unregistered marriage does not get pension rights. I recently had to help a client whose mother-in-law was using the fact that my client had no proof of her marriage to prevent the coroner from releasing the body of her deceased son to his widow. In another case I had to urgently fax a judge in Syria to help a British woman who had been imprisoned for *zina* (unlawful sexual intercourse). Her unborn child was due to be taken away at birth, because her husband had stranded her in Syria and taken their marriage certificate with him, leaving her unable to prove she was married. If her marriage had been registered, the Syrian court would have been able to see that and release her. I also had a client who, along with her four children, was made homeless upon widowhood when her in-laws refused to accept the fact of her marriage. With a legal marriage, all of these women would have been protected under English and international law.

People are surprised to learn that it is harder nowadays to get out of a UK mobile phone contract than it is to leave an Islamic marriage. Where a mobile phone contract might bind you in for twenty-four months, an unregistered *nikah* means you can simply leave at any time, with no repercussions. Until we require marriage to be legally enforceable, as it is in all Muslim countries, we will be allowing widespread misery because without an official piece of paper, there is nothing legally binding in place to protect you. When people realize this, whether Muslim or non-Muslim, they are shocked. The remarkable thing is that our politicians do not seem to know the legal position, and neither do many lawyers. If they do not know what the law says, then we are doing a hopeless job of protecting people.

Back in 2010, I spoke at a round table meeting with the then Home Secretary, Theresa May. She asked for data to prove that the number of unregistered marriages was increasing. When I said there was none and no one was likely to cooperate in government research, yet the rates were growing exponentially, she asked the Ministry of Justice to set up the Muslim Marriages Working Group to investigate. We gathered national statistics and issued a report in 2012 recommending that (a) a campaign of awareness was launched, and (b) the law was changed to require compulsory registration. But after years of work, the report was politely received but ignored by the government. I also gave evidence to the Law Commission, which published a report in 2015 recommending a wholesale review of marriage law.[8] That was also ignored.

Yet I was still receiving calls and emails daily with what my team called 'another *nikah* horror story'. The issue had gone unaddressed long enough and I had to do something. For too long, I had been dismayed to see that Muslim women had become their own worst enemies in accessing their legal rights. They were either unaware that they were unprotected in an unregistered marriage, or uncaring until it was too late. Innocent children were suffering, and outcomes for families were poor when they were becoming reliant on welfare benefits and the children were fatherless.

So I was inspired to start the ROM campaign through sheer frustration. Happily, in the last year, it has gained traction and had a lot of media attention. We have done a series of nationwide road shows and social media campaigns, and in November 2017 a prime-time one-hour documentary, *The Truth about Muslim Marriage*, aired on Channel 4, which had followed my clients and me for a year. The channel also carried out a survey of 1,000 women nationwide, which found that nearly two thirds of Muslim marriages are unregistered.[9] In March 2018, the government published a Green Paper that endorsed the two-pronged approach of the ROM campaign: (a) to make it compulsory to register marriages, and (b) to raise awareness of the perils of not doing so.[10] Finally, years of effort appear to be paying off.

The ROM campaign has not met resistance from Muslims and has enjoyed widespread support. But hardliners still believe that Islam is all you need. This lip service to Islam is especially problematic because the true scholarly narrative is that an Islamic marriage is an enforceable contract, in which a husband protects his wife and children financially. If he is not doing that, he has not honoured the contract. Leading imams have publicly confirmed this Islamic narrative of marriage and are supporters of my campaign. They endorse my view that a *nikah* is being turned into a purely religious ceremony, when in Islam it is a contract between two people in front of God, and not a sacrament (a Church ceremony). Islam is fully protective of its women and children. It will not allow them to be dependent on the State or their own family. Over 1,400 years ago, Islam introduced compulsory legal marriage to protect women and children in the event of death or divorce. But we have gone back to the pre-Islamic days of *jahiliyat* (ignorance) when women had no worth and were grateful if a man looked after them. We have dispensed with our God-given rights, and our men are behaving with impunity.

It is now emerging that African evangelical churches are also showing low rates of marriage registration, and misogyny appears to be a common denominator. Muslims say to me, 'Women have never had these legal rights; English law is giving them too much.' So, my campaign goes back to its source: Islamic justice. Once you strip away patriarchal culture and tradition, you get back to this fundamental point very quickly. It is a common misconception that a Muslim woman cannot be autonomous. In Islam, a woman can keep her property, her earnings, and even her own name after marriage. Although in an Arabic, Asian or African context, a man has full control over his wife, Islam asks women to stand on their own feet within a marriage contract. If she wants *tafweed* (an equal right to divorce), she can put it in the marriage contract. If she does not want her husband to take another wife, she makes that a condition. If she wants maintenance after divorce, she can stipulate that to protect herself. The list goes on. But today women are not even asking for their basic human rights because it is considered unfeminine and immodest. The Quran provides these rights, and we need to go back to that source. So many women find it a relief to hear this from me and feel empowered.

It is incredible that Islamic marriage laws have been completely misinterpreted by Muslims themselves. Yet I understand why it has happened. Human nature would rather avoid dramatic change. In early Islam in seventh-century Arabia, Muslim women were feisty and unafraid to fight for their rights. With the passing of the centuries, their dramatic progress stagnated and stalled, causing them to regress. Women need to reclaim their rightful legacy by educating themselves, as is a duty under Islam. I have been heartened to find that men are keen to support my campaign and that they are often the best sponsors of women, helping them to achieve their rights when they are too fearful to do so for themselves. We must remember, however, that this is not just about women; it is about human rights. I have had men cry in front of me after their wives have taken their life savings to invest in a house that was bought in the wife's sole name as she was the bigger earner. After having an unregistered *nikah* and leaving them, they knew there was little chance of the man winning a civil contract claim against them.

The good news is that things now seem to be changing. People are telling me they are having their marriages registered, and imams are refusing to carry out *nikahs* without a legal marriage first. We now await the result of data analysis that will tell us whether the trend has been halted and is reversing.

In January 2018, I was given an OBE* by the Queen in her New Year's Honours for 'Services to the Protection of Women and Children in Unregistered Marriages'. This has brought greater recognition to the ROM campaign. I have set up a National Working Group to carry out a two-year nationwide awareness campaign, and the government is actively engaging with me in securing change.

In June 2018, I launched my own law firm, Aina Khan Law, focusing on complex and international family law. I have trained teams at law firms around the country to deal with unregistered marriage cases and the ROM website provides information. It is clear ROM cannot continue to run as a voluntary body and has to formalize its structure. The next step is for us to raise funding from the government and private investors. We also actively

---

* Officer of the Order of the British Empire.

welcome supporters and volunteers who will assist us globally via video and the latest tech. With ROM as a beacon, I look forward to better outcomes and a brighter future for Muslim families abroad, who are increasingly suffering the same issues. With lawyers, activists, bloggers and more, we can together ensure the success of the ROM campaign and empower women all over the world, who look to the UK to show the way ahead for Muslim communities.

---

1   'Patterns of Membership', compiled for the Yearly Meeting of the Religious Society of Friends (Quakers) in Britain (4–7 May 2018), https://quaker-prod.s3.eu-west-1.amazonaws.com/store/c825a0871eaaee20a290b33c5b2b25baf8cb306246ef01582658 2885f14b

2   '2011 Census analysis: Ethnicity and religion of the non-UK born population in England and Wales', ONS (18 June 2015), https://www.ons.gov.uk/peoplepopulationandcommunity/culturalidentity/ethnicity/articles/2011censusanalysisethnicity andreligionofthenonukbornpopulationinenglandandwales/2015-06-18#religion

3   'Marriages and civil partnerships in the UK', https://www.gov.uk/marriages-civil-partnerships/what-you-need-to-do

4   https://www.registerourmarriage.org

5   http://www.shariahcouncil.org/

6   '"Am I bothered?": The Relevance of Religious Courts to a Civil Judge', keynote address by The Honourable Mr Justice McFarlane at Cardiff Law School (18 May 2011), http://www.law.cf.ac.uk/clr/Hon.%20Mr%20Justice%20McFarlane_%20The%20Relevance%20of%20Religious%20Courts%20to%20a%20Civil%20Judge.pdf

7   'Marriages in England and Wales: 2015', ONS (28 February 2018), https://www.ons.gov.uk/peoplepopulationandcommunity/birthsdeathsandmarriages/marriagecohabitationandcivilpartnerships/bulletins/marriagesinenglandandwalesprovisional/2015#statisticians-comment

8   'Getting Married: A Scoping Paper', report by the Law
    Commission (17 December 2015), https://s3-eu-west-2.
    amazonaws.com/lawcom-prod-storage-11jsxou24uy7q/
    uploads/2015/12/Executive-summary-Getting-Married.pdf
9   'New Channel 4 survey reveals The Truth About Muslim
    Marriage', Channel 4 (20 November 2017), http://www.channel4.
    com/info/press/news/new-channel-4-survey-reveals-the-truth-
    about-muslim-marriage
10 'Integrated Communities Strategy Green Paper', HM Government
    (March 2018), https://assets.publishing.service.gov.uk/government/
    uploads/system/uploads/attachment_data/file/696993/Integrated_
    Communities_Strategy.pdf

Not *Just* a Black Muslim Woman

Raifa Rafiq

I am a Black Muslim Woman. What can such a statement tell you about me? Other than that my home is the central intersection in a Venn diagram of oppression. Navigating that niche space can and has often proved difficult for me. I have lived and read the double burden of the Black Woman, but to add the Maggi cube that is 'Muslim' is to confuse and make complex a broth that has been brewing violently inside me ever since I knew of myself.

Becoming is something that I could have done without. On the crisp winter night of 25 January 1999, I landed in England from Zanzibar, a small island off the coast of mainland Tanzania. Up until that point I was always just Raifa, a chatty chirpy five-year-old, surrounded and loved by a normal family, and navigating a fairly routine life of school, madrasa, private tuition and a far too early bedtime. I was sure of who I was and where I fitted in the small world around me. My identity was unique to me but it was also familiar. I was normal. But on the night I landed at Heathrow airport, I became black. It started before I even got off the plane. During the flight I was taught by an elderly couple sitting next to me to eat something called 'spaghetti' with a fork, then as we disembarked, I was given a blanket because my aunt had underestimated the cold in England. In an instant, I felt like the wrong jigsaw piece being forced into a space that didn't have the measurements to accommodate me. All the dimensions were wrong. In this new country, the people did not look like me or sound like me. The weather was playing havoc with my body and the displacement made me feel as though a few bones in my spine had broken free so that I instantly cowered and became smaller. A volcano had erupted inside me and I was dismantling.

White people – up until the moment I landed in England – were foreigners who would come to Zanzibar and take pictures. We would point at them in their bikinis when my father took my siblings, cousins and me to the beach every Sunday. They were in brochures and the news. They represented something far, far away. They were *other*. But now I was in England, my skin had caught fire, and I was aware of my blackness. Nothing demands self-consciousness like the feeling of difference. Difference roots you to the ground.

What I soon discovered, however, when I reached school, was that Black culture in Britain was cool. And so were the black kids. We were in vogue. There is no doubt that Black culture and Black identity is commercially exploited and moulded to profit everyone who is not black: to be black in Britain is to see your life used as a prop in a pantomime that you cannot direct. Everyone wants to be black but nobody wants to live black. And yet, I embraced it. Being a young black girl was to have 'flavour'. According to my teachers I was 'loud', 'disruptive' and 'sassy', and, realizing that I would neither understand nor be understood by the white girls, I naturally gravitated towards the black girls and boys. It was a sort of comfort, I suppose, assuming that these other people were similar to me in some way.

Notwithstanding this, I was always the sore thumb in my group of black friends. I looked different, because the other thing I had brought with me from Zanzibar, without realizing it, was my religion. I had been born Muslim, but in Zanzibar Islam was a way of life that didn't require a hijab to highlight its presence. Here in England it did. By the time I was ten, I had started wearing a hijab and long skirts like every other woman in my family. I dressed like a practising Muslim without realizing that to be visibly Muslim is to make a statement that you should be ready to defend and justify. I consider now all the think pieces Muslim women write in defence of our decision to wear the hijab, and wonder if they are just a response to childhood experiences very much like my own, when nine-year-old Sarah Smith asked me on that first day of the new school year, 'Why are you wearing that on your head?' Reasons for deciding to wear hijab aside, I remember the absolute terror of entering school with new head gear and my sick apprehension that I'd lose some friends – as if I wasn't different enough, having spent the past few years learning how to speak a foreign language.

Though I thought I stood out amongst my friends, I was lucky enough not to be made to feel different. And yet, whilst I felt like a part of the group of young black girls at school, there was a fragment of me I was never able to share. If someone sneezed I would say bless you, but under my breath I would tentatively mumble *alhamdullilah* for them and then *yarhamuk Allah* (may Allah have mercy on you). I did it silently, of course; I didn't want people thinking I was weird, and God forbid I start having to explain what I was saying.

I recall a particular incident in my teenage years that will stay with me forever. I was around fifteen years old and it was by all standards a normal school day. A fight had broken out in the corridors of the East London academy I went to and I got mixed in the ruckus of the crowd. I was small for my age, five foot, and I was soon being crushed inside a sea of people. I became so flustered and scared that I started shouting at the top of my lungs *–subhanallah!* – over and over again. One of my friends pulled me to the side, looked at me with genuine fright, and asked, 'Are you all right? Are you speaking in tongues or something?' How was she to know that *subhanallah* is our version of 'oh my God', and how was I to begin explaining that to her? I told her I was fine, said I was sorry, laughed and shrugged the episode off to put her at ease. I realized then that I was apologizing for something that I said at home every day. It was part of who I was, and yet I was ashamed to show it, to make others uncomfortable for having to deal with and witness my difference.

Because the fact was, in the world I now found myself in, being Black and Muslim simply wasn't compatible: 'Muslim' was an identity that the South Asian community had taken sole custody of. Every Eid I'd request to wear *salwar kameezes* and saris so I could look the part, and yet 'you don't look Muslim' was a recurring statement I had to refute from fellow Muslim kids. When corporate boardrooms want to increase the number of Muslim employees to fulfil diversity quotas, I assume they wouldn't go looking for a black Muslim man or a non-hijab-wearing black Muslimah. No, to be Muslim you must look it, and looking Muslim is still to look

South Asian. Balancing these dichotomous identities that seemed to quite literally repel each other was a task that simply proved too difficult. And remember, at school being black was cool. The Asian kids, that group who 'owned' being Muslim, weren't. I had a decision to make, and I chose to be black at school and Muslim at home. I would sometimes wear my scarf in a different way and call my hijab a 'head wrap', removing any theological undertones.

And there was another pair of clashing identities to contend with too. I was a first-generation immigrant – I needed to learn to be East African at home but British outside, a Britishness I knew not to bring inside the house lest I be told I was becoming too western. The whole thing was exhausting and ultimately, the small decisions I made as a child to ensure I fitted into the different places I found myself actually meant that I had no place, no intersection that I could call home. Nowhere I truly belonged. Back in Zanzibar I had belonged, and I knew belonging was a wonderful thing. Belonging is like a trampoline. It is having the awareness that no matter how high you jump, how many risks you take, there is a place down there that will absorb the force of your fall should you ever come crashing down. Belonging will propel you back up from such a fall. Higher.

The trouble of my belonging and the trials in my becoming inform a problem that we know all too well. Stereotypes. We are all governed by certain stereotypes that may or may not pertain to a truth in our own lived experiences, but to be a young Black Muslim girl is to tolerate and balance stereotypes that have no business being together.

Whilst being Muslim and black around other black people was 'different', I never felt discriminated against or unwanted. On the other hand, being Muslim and black around non-black Muslims has always been much more uncomfortable. I was very aware of the anti-blackness in Muslim communities, be it through family anecdotes of things that my relatives had encountered, or stories from close black friends who weren't allowed to meet their Asian boyfriends' parents due to the dis-approval of their race. Whilst Islam teaches you to love everyone under the religion like your own family, it seems like such a lesson is lost on those who choose to put cultural differences ahead of religious teachings.

Whiteness, and its distribution amongst the colonies (not to mention the historic colonial association of blackness with 'savagery'), was an instrumental appar-atus for its standing within the imperial project, and today it clearly still remains a gnawing influence that the diaspora holds onto and uses to punish itself. We are brothers and sisters so long as we keep our distance. We are brothers and sisters so long as we do not marry into their families and bring our black culture and practices into their homes. The closer you are to whiteness or fairness in the Muslim community (as with any other non-white community), the closer you are to being the perfect Muslim. Take the Arabs, for example. Whilst many would see them as the archetypal Muslims because the Prophet Mohammed (pbuh), the man who first received God's word, was an Arab, I believe that part of the fact that the Arab Muslim face has become the acceptable face of Islam is to do with the paleness of their skin, their proximity to whiteness. And then there's the sexism embedded in so much Muslim culture. Men see the 'violence' of my race and the 'weakness' of my gender.

How, then, can a Black Muslim Woman, someone

who can call home many places but equally not sit comfortably anywhere, find a way to capture the stereotypes and the ideas imposed by others on her and recalibrate them so that they better represent who she truly is? It is an arduous task and frankly one that is not my responsibility. Religion, race and gender interact so intimately that to try to unpack one is to intrude on the other. It is impossible to have a conversation about how I am perceived as a Muslim without trespassing on my existence as a woman, and my existence as a woman cannot be isolated from my race, as being a black woman is very different to just being a woman. To begin taking up space and debunking the stereotypes pertaining to being a Black Muslim Woman, you have to take a lesson from a hideous little book, Sun Tzu's *The Art of War*: 'If you know the enemy and you know yourself, you need not fear the result of a hundred battles. If you know yourself but not the enemy, for every victory gained you will suffer a defeat. If you know neither the enemy nor yourself, you will succumb in every battle.'[1]

I do not believe that to know your enemy is to win. Black people have so intricately known the white man and we are still systematically hindered in the supposedly post-colonial world in which we exist. However, to know your enemy as a Black Muslim Woman is to see that the slight overlaps in the diagram of oppression are not the doing of the oppressed peoples. To know the enemy is to equip yourself with the understanding that we have been fed the idea that we must all seek to be close to the White Man. The closer we are to him, the better we will be. And what person is further from the (secular) White Man than the Black Muslim Woman? It is unsurprising, then, that she feels the weight of all those eyes. This race to proximity explains why, even though

Islam says that its followers should accept a black Muslim as their own, the trend is in the opposite direction. What we have here is racial, theological and gender advancement: the survival of the fittest, where the current fittest is the secular White Man. If 'social evolution' means only the fittest survive, then (a) it favours the secular White Man due to the societal infrastructures that support him and inevitably leave the Black Muslim Woman at the back of the queue, and (b) it allows whiteness to be perceived as transient, as something that can be achieved or improved; and so a competition ensues between those who are not the White Man. They must run as fast as they can to reach the unreachable: the White Man in the distance, the ever-moving finish line.

Nonetheless, whilst for years the Black Muslim Woman has been at the back of the queue, the fact that racial whiteness (and all its associated social qualities) has been successful due to social evolution also exhibits its weakness – the fragility of its position. As society changes, the goal posts are likewise shifting, and now we see the conversation changing. Perhaps now we can start to decipher, realign and move those foundations so that attention is on us. And if they do not give us the mic to speak, we build our own stage – I was never a fan of their stage anyway; how correct it stood, how sturdy and mute, how cold it was.

So, Black Muslim Women need to take up space. To be unapologetically Muslim, unapologetically black and unapologetically women. A few weeks ago I walked into Leytonstone tube station and saw a TFL conductor who was a black Muslim hijabi woman. I was shocked and then ashamed that such a thing should surprise me. If we do not see such women in everyday roles they cannot challenge our perceptions. I am tired of being part of panels of Muslim women in front of other Muslim women. One person shaking the table at work isn't going to be enough for people to get 'comfortable' with the idea of who we are. We are not the ones that have to change, but expecting that floppy-haired white boy you know to take action might mean you're in for a long old wait.

Therefore, I call for a dance when the White Man's gaze is on us. A shimmy. An impenitent and defiant shake of the waist, a tectonic shift where we stop apologizing for who we are, where we stop prioritizing the comfort of others, where we stop placating and appeasing and upholding the status quo that strengthens our own shackles. I call for so much noise-making that it is impossible to ignore us. I call for us not to seek to 'break' stereotypes, but to see the magic of our normal.

When approached to write this essay, I knew that I wanted to write about my story of being a Black Muslim Woman in Britain. On thinking deeper, however, I queried my own decision to squeeze all that I am into this trinity of labels. Black. Muslim. Woman. Surely, when people ask me who I am I simply say, 'I am Raifa.' I go on to say that I am a trainee lawyer at one of the best law firms in the world. I tell them that I am a writer. I talk about my love of literature, my amazing podcast and fierce feminism. I do not simply say, 'I am a Black Muslim Woman.' But this is what others say of me, and in pre-empting the identity that the world gives me, I have internalized it. I am all of these things, but my identity is the intangible part of me that is multifaceted, multidimensional and complex. Nuanced, like how we allow young white women to be. My identity is the late-night YouTube binges, my Google search history and the fact that I can't sleep with the door open. My identity is the fact that I cry when it's cold and I can't function without my morning coffee. My identity is my obsession with Bollywood movies and making lists that distress me because no list is ever entirely ticked off. My identity is waking up in the middle of the night to clean my house. It is my insomnia and my anxiety. My identity is my fierce belief that feminism can change the world. My identity is my ambitions and my tenacious desire to succeed. It is my love of family, my absolute annoyance at being persuaded to cook when I could just use Uber Eats. My identity is overflowing and cannot be squeezed into the three words that others use so carelessly. Black. Muslim. Woman. That is all that I am to you.

I'd like to ensure that, should I have a daughter, she could be Muslim and black Tanzanian and British wherever she is. But most importantly, when she is asked who she is, I'd like for her to respond with her name, her likes and her dislikes, I'd like for her to respond with the things that make her heart warm and the dreams she has for her future. And maybe, just maybe, when our existence becomes the norm and not just a trend or a difference, we can sit comfortably in the intersection of that Venn diagram that I call 'home'.

---

1   *Sun Tzu on the Art of War*, translated from the Chinese by Lionel Giles, M.A. (1910) https://sites.ualberta.ca/~enoch/Readings/The_Art_Of_War.pdf

Between Submission and Threat:

The British State's Contradictory Relationship with Muslim Women

Malia Bouattia

The British state has a somewhat contradictory relationship with Muslim women. On the one hand, it plays a considerable role in our demonization by issuing policy after policy – from the Prevent strategy* and Schedule 7†to the policing of the hijab in schools by Ofsted – that actively institutionalizes our oppression. On the other it proclaims to be the saviour that 'shines a light' on our oppression within the Muslim community. Muslim women, we are told, must be rescued, celebrated, and brought into the fold.

---

* Policy introduced in the UK in 2003 as part of the government's counter-terrorism approach, with the aim of preventing the radicalization of individuals to terrorism.

† Under Section 7 of the Terrorism Act 2000, police have powers to stop, question, search and detain people entering or leaving the UK

This 'relationship', however, exists on the basis of our own voices remaining absent. We are not part of the conversation. Make no mistake – our existence in British society is important, but the relationship is dependent on us being both visible and silent: on being talked about but never invited into the discussion. We serve both as targets of official Islamophobic policies – helpfully depicted in turn as dangerous, refusing to integrate, or allowing extremism to fester within Muslim households – and as props in dominant Islamophobic discourses, in which the British state moves to police, survey, or discipline Muslim men in order to 'save' us from the dangers of a supposed specifically Muslim patriarchy. It is this contradictory relationship between Muslim women and the state, perpetually oscillating between victimization and criminalization, that I aim to explore.

In this essay, I will refer to 'the state' rather than to individual governments, ministries, media organizations or authorities. Indeed, although specific actions are connected to the decisions of specific individuals, the day-to-day experience of Muslim women (and Muslim communities in general) has been shaped in much the same way by different authorities. The processes I want to look at are part of a general approach to Muslim communities driven by the state, as a collection of institutions, since the onset of the so-called War on Terror in the early 2000s. Not one in a series of different political parties or prime ministers has ever radically altered the way Muslims are depicted: outside the British collective, a threat to the vague concept of 'British values', and ever-suspicious bodies to be controlled. The issue is an institutional one that facilitates our dehumanization and targeting.

Over the last few decades different governments have, when trying to strengthen their credentials in the face of falling popularity, found it helpful to take aim at Muslim women. Jack Straw, for example, triggered a national debate on the possibility of a burqa/veil ban after criticizing Muslim women in his surgery for wearing Islamic attire.[1] Similarly, David Cameron's criticism that Muslim women's English language skills were not up to scratch allowed him to present himself as a defender of British values when he was put under pressure by the right wing of the Conservative Party and the growth of UKIP.[2] It was a statement he made after cutting £400 million from the English language teaching budget,[3] cutting back welfare services including women's shelters,[4] and shutting down the youth and community centres[5] that often provide working-class Muslim women with a much-needed break from daily isolation with their children in the home. Both MPs' statements aimed to demonize our apparent inability to integrate and act within British society, *and* relied on it: Muslim women's voices are absent from the spaces that produce the narratives sustaining our oppression.

Much the same can be said when we look at counterterrorism and anti-radicalization projects. From the Blair years onwards, a growing array of policies and governmental guidelines have targeted, criminalized, and othered Muslim communities. The Prevent strategy, with its focus on so-called radicalization, 'non-violent extremism', and a pre-criminal space,[6] has been developed and intensified continuously from the early 2000s onwards, with a striking continuity from Labour to Tory governments. The disciplining of Muslim women as the supposed source of radicalization in the home through the threat (and application) of separating children from their mothers or the threat of extradition, as explained brilliantly by Nisha Kapoor in her book *Deport, Deprive, Extradite*, has also remained a constant from government to government.[7]

Indeed, as Kapoor and many others have shown, the growing body of counter-terrorism legislation has worked to criminalize Muslim communities and roll back civil liberties more broadly across society. The Prevent strategy is a good example of this process. Prevent aims to identify individuals who are being radicalized and might be susceptible to becoming terrorists. It does not do so on the basis of identifying – as with other forms of policing – potential criminal activity or intent, but instead it focuses on ideas and ideological commitments. It effectively creates a category of 'thought crimes'. In 2015, it became a legal duty[8] for all public-sector employees to report on their 'service users' (students, patients, etc.) for any signs of radicalization, including critiquing British foreign policy, supporting Palestine, an apparent 'desire for change', changing groups of friends, or – unbelievably – criticizing Prevent. Unsurprisingly, Muslims, despite making up just over 5 per cent of the British population, have made up more than half of those referred under Prevent guidelines, and increasingly groups such as anti-fracking campaigners and Palestine solidarity activists have also been targeted.[9]

The message, once again, is clear: Muslims are considered guilty of criminal potential without demonstrating any criminal intent. The act of expressing oppositional political opinions or behaving in an (ill-defined) suspicious way is enough to make us guilty of (potential) crimes. Our very existence, let alone our actions and our opinions, are then politicized by the state and we are rendered suspect and silenced the moment we protest.

It is important to recognize this backdrop and this political climate when discussing the current situation of Muslim women in the UK, because it is within this space that the politicization of a number of Muslim women, often from second- or third-generation immigrant backgrounds, has taken place. Indeed, in the face of growing state targeting of Muslim communities in general, and Muslim women in particular, many of us have been dragged into the political sphere, whether by choice or not.

However, becoming politically active, speaking up, and getting organized threatens the very authorities that continue to rely on our hyper-visibility *as well as* our silence. When Muslim women choose to take a stand and vocalize our opinions, there are always consequences to our dissent – especially because it flips the orientalist caricature of a passive, repressed woman being held hostage by the men in her community.

My experiences throughout the time that I served as an officer of the National Union of Students (NUS) were a small taste of the reception that awaits Muslim women when they choose to take up leadership roles – especially when they are on a platform of social justice.

I was elected as the Black Students' Officer in the NUS for two consecutive terms, from 2014–16. As such, I represented over a million students of African, Asian, Arab, Caribbean and South American descent, across the country. Within months of taking up the position, I found myself in the eye of a racist and misogynist media storm. A motion had been put forward that asked the NUS to condemn ISIS and support the Kurdish struggle for independence in Iraq and Syria. It also called on students to identify and boycott those 'found to support ISIS'. Given the existing Islamophobic political climate and the ongoing targeting of Muslims on campuses through Prevent (Muslim students were regularly accused of being, or supporting, terrorists), and in the absence of any other obvious objectives for a student boycott, the motion worried me. I raised my concerns and requested that the union consider re-writing the motion alongside Kurdish students, in order to avoid leaving any hostages to fortune.

It sounds simple enough and would – you'd think – have passed without a hitch, but needless to say my words were used against me, and suddenly I was being depicted as an ISIS sympathizer across the national media (ironically demonstrating the very point I raised concerns about in the meeting). A Muslim woman in an influential position 'supporting ISIS' makes a great headline, and the truth was secondary. Fascists and racists worldwide, plus the former EDL leader Tommy Robinson, took to attacking me on social media and in the press. I received countless death threats that led to police involvement, and had to move back to my parents' home for safety.

It was my first taste of the levels of harassment that could come out of total fabrication, and of the reality that important media platforms were prepared to run with this false story despite the mounting threats to my life and family. No wonder so many Muslim women assume that if they choose to take action, speak out, or decide to take the UK government and racist institutions to task, a public onslaught awaits them.

Then, in April 2016, I was elected the first Muslim and woman of colour president of the NUS. My election was significant, not only because of who I am and what that represents, but also because of the platform on which I stood. Indeed, with the support of the liberation groups and the left wing of the union, this was the first time in a generation that an openly socialist candidate was elected as president of the NUS. I had advocated for free education, solidarity with the struggle for freedom of the Palestinians, and support for the thousands of students that were campaigning to tackle institutionalized racism in universities and colleges across the UK. I also proposed to take the NUS in a direction focused on campaigning and allying with other unions and social justice groups. All of these approaches were unheard of within the union and often actively opposed by its existing leadership. In many ways, this was a deeply exciting period.

However, I quickly discovered – in fact on the very same day my election was announced – that my platform would remain in the shadows of who I was; or, I should say, who I was depicted to be. I was branded an anti-Semite, an ISIS supporter, and a terrorist sympathizer within hours of the result. Despite repeated statements, clarifications, and public explanations of my beliefs and politics, sound bites and selective quotes were played over and over again across the press for the duration of my presidency. I had gone from being the first left-wing, anti-racist, activist president of the NUS elected in a generation, to being depicted as the very opposite: an oppressive, racist, and reactionary Muslim seizing the lead role in an important institution.

It was the hardest year of my life. Not only did I have to deal with the frustration of being presented as something I was not, but the tone and nature of the attacks also made any reasoned discussion impossible. I had been judged and found guilty before even stepping into the role, before even opening my mouth. It was all well and good to celebrate migrants, women of colour, or Muslims in the NUS until one became its president and had opinions that the establishment did not agree with. I was reminded of my place in society: I was to be talked about without ever being able to intervene, the object rather than the subject of the conversation.

My story offers a small insight into the treatment reserved for Muslim women when they don't 'put themselves out there' through the narrow 'good Muslim' framework offered by the state. I was confronted daily with the fact that refusing to comply meant that I was automatically written into a series of assumptions, patterns, stereotypes, and prejudices. As a Muslim woman who refused to stick to the acceptable lines and positions, what I actually stood for, believed, or did mattered little. What the structures of power dictated about what my refusal actually meant – that I was a terrorist, a racist, secretly reactionary, etc. – on the other hand, did not need proof. For those in power, just to say it was enough. It fitted perfectly in a well-rehearsed script.

There is, of course, always an alternative. The British political establishment is happy to present a model Muslim woman – a single expression of Muslim female identity that is acceptable. The newly appointed leader for the Commission for Countering Extremism (CCE), Sara Khan, is the most recent example of this. The message is clear: a non-hijab-wearing right-wing Muslim woman who demonizes both critical and left-wing Muslims, and Muslims who seem 'too religious' or at least not religious in the right way, is acceptable in the public sphere. Everybody else should change or remain silent. Muslims who reinforce the racist idea that there is a

'Muslim threat' and believe that our community should be monitored are the example we should all follow.

If the policing of Muslim women does not come in the form of character assassination then it seems that the state will attempt to infiltrate and control political spaces where Muslim women are seeking empowerment and organizing against the inequalities that surround them. In 2013, the NUS launched a leadership training initiative known as I Will Lead the Way for Muslim Women. The decision came out of the ongoing frustration within the student community that the men who led our organizations were so often celebrated whilst the women were given the brunt of the legwork and expected to be neither heard nor seen in public arenas. This new project aimed to address the reasons why Muslim women were not putting themselves forward as front-facing leaders within their student unions, or running in local elections.

Many of the Muslim women who would go on to lead efforts against Prevent, and to campaign in solidarity with refugees, against the privatization of higher education, and on intersectional women's liberation and so much more, passed through the training provided by NUS and this initiative. But then, in 2016, it came to light that the project was funded by the Home Office, and was linked to their targeted counter-terrorism work. This again illustrates the dual approach by state agencies in dealing with Muslim women: on the one hand, repressive policies such as Prevent target our political expression; on the other hand, and at the same time, our political spaces are funded by the very bodies criminalizing us in a bid to justify their actions through the prism of women's liberation. We are both victims of state violence and the very objects used to justify the violence we suffer. It is noteworthy that the funding of this particular project could easily be used to strengthen the narrative of the British state supporting Muslim women to overcome the yoke imposed on us by Muslim men.

In some ways the intrusion into and attempted co-option of a space that was supposed to serve as a platform for dismantling the multiple oppressions many of us face – racism, sexism, xenophobia – was unsurprising if we once again reflect on the historical orientalizing of the Muslim woman by western imperialist nations. In *A Dying Colonialism* (1959) Frantz Fanon reflects on France's colonial approach to the indigenous women: 'If we want to destroy the structure of Algerian society, its capacity for resistance, we must first of all conquer the women; we must go and find them behind the veil where they hide themselves and in the houses where the men keep them out of sight.'

In the same way as French colonialism used the myth of the 'civilizing mission' to legitimize the occupation of Algeria, during which they staged 'unveiling' campaigns for women wearing the traditional *haik* (the Algerian niqab) in an attempt to 'liberate' them from the repressive patriarchal grip of their men, the British in Egypt saw women as the entry point to disciplining the 'native household'. Timothy Mitchell, in *Colonising Egypt*, explains how colonial officers drew 'a link between the country's "moral inferiority" and the status of its women'. He explains that they regularly came back to the argument that 'the retarded development of the nation corresponded [. . .] to the retarded development of the Egyptian woman'.[10] Indeed, the British consul-general of Egypt Lord Cromer wrote in the early 1900s: 'The position of women in Egypt . . . is a fatal obstacle to the attainment of that elevation of thought and character which should accompany the introduction of European civilization.'[11] Contemporary British practice remains highly reminiscent of this colonial approach. It sees Muslim women as the key entry point for the repressive apparatus unleashed against our community under the cover of fighting terrorism, radicalization, and 'non-violent extremism'.

The imperialist obsession with the Muslim woman being simultaneously a source of intelligence with regard to the threat posed by the mythical barbarism of the racialized Muslim man, the key to disciplining the Muslim household, and the victim to be saved from her male counterpart (which therefore justifies state violence and surveillance) is still an underlying ideological foundation in the continued War on Terror that sustains the marginalization and oppression of Muslim women. The recent Ofsted decision to target schoolgirls who wear the hijab is a further reminder of this trend.[12] It turns out – once more – that 'freedom to choose' is limited to making the right kind of choices. And it also reminds us of the point about silence I've already made: whichever of these different approaches the state is taking at any given time, the Muslim woman is required to remain the silent object of policy, always to be talked about without ever being invited to participate in the conversation.

This treatment of Muslim women by the British state is dangerous because it generates division and distrust, and reinforces misogyny as well as undermining the ability of Muslim women to address sexist tendencies within their communities. It tells us that the state is an anti-sexist force working against male Muslims and their aggressive patriarchy. It asks women to choose between their community and the state, between their identity as

Muslims and their identity as women. But this is a false dichotomy. While it should be immediately obvious that, as misogyny exists in wider society, so it will inevitably exist within the Muslim community, it is also important to remember that, in the same way any man can make the decision to fight misogyny, so can a Muslim man. It seems silly to spell this out, but there is no doubt that it is unfortunately necessary in the current circumstances.

The deplorable campaign by FEMEN, a group that called for an 'International Topless Jihad' day by bearing their breasts outside mosques across Europe in 2013 to supposedly 'free' Muslim women, was an example of women's rights and demands being mobilized as part of the sustained attack against the Muslim community. Again, Muslim women were being asked to choose between being 'freed women' and their community, always imagined as male, patriarchal, and repressive. The state and groups like FEMEN are not allies of Muslim women, and therefore cannot achieve their liberation, but this sort of campaign damages those Muslim women who are trying to tackle misogyny within their communities. Actions like these risk causing women who raise concerns and demands, and organize against internal misogyny, to be depicted as carrying an external assault to the heart of their own people: they are perceived to be serving as extensions of Islamophobic policies and campaigns. Suddenly Muslim women are depicted as both the enemy within and the enemy without.

The question then remains: what is to be done? Is there a potentially productive or progressive relationship possible between our communities, our struggles, and the state? While, as a thought experiment, the idea might be tempting, the reality on the ground does not point in that direction. The state as an institution cannot be an effective ally for our struggles or our campaigns, let alone for our liberation, as long as it deems Muslim communities to be suspect, dangerous, and in need of control and surveillance. It cannot develop constructive relationships with communities that it homogenizes and represses, nor can it offer a route out of oppression to women who bear the brunt of its oppressive policies. The question of Islamophobia today is primarily one that is encouraged and legislated by politicians, institutionalized by state agencies, and reproduced in spaces of education, employment, housing, and health. It is one that will require Muslims to build broad alliances with others – unions, community groups, social justice campaigners – who are concerned about the rise of racism, the undermining of civil liberties, and the growth of discriminatory policies. It is these people who will serve as our allies in the struggle ahead.

---

1   Jack Straw, 'I felt uneasy talking to someone I couldn't see', *Guardian* (6 October 2006), https://www.theguardian.com/commentisfree/2006/oct/06/politics.uk

2   Madeleine Bunting, 'Cameron and Muslim women: a new twist on an old colonial story', *Guardian* (22 January 2016), https://www.theguardian.com/commentisfree/2016/jan/22/david-cameron-muslim-women

3   Bunting (2016)

4   Jon Stone, 'David Cameron begged to spare refuges for domestic violence victims from cuts', *Independent* (11 May 2016), https://www.independent.co.uk/news/uk/politics/david-cameron-begged-to-spare-refuges-for-domestic-violence-victims-from-cuts-a7024306.html

5   'Services for young people', www.parliament.uk (23 June 2011), https://publications.parliament.uk/pa/cm201012/cmselect/cmeduc/744/4403.htm

6 '*Prevent* duty guidance', HM Government (2015), https://www.legislation.gov.uk/ukdsi/2015/9780111133309/pdfs/ukdsiod_9780111133309_en.pdf

7 Nisha Kapoor, *Deport, Deprive, Extradite* (London, 2018)

8 Counter-Terrorism and Security Act 2015, Legislation.gov.uk (2015), http://www.legislation.gov.uk/ukpga/2015/6/contents/enacted

9 For more on this, see Karma Nabulsi, 'Don't Go to the Doctor: Snitching on Students' in *London Review of Books* (2017), 39:10, 27–28, https://www.lrb.co.uk/v39/n10/karma-nabulsi/dont-go-to-the-doctor, or the Open Society Justice Initiative's report 'Eroding Trust: The UK's Prevent Counter-Extremism Strategy in Health and Education' (October 2016), https://www.opensocietyfoundations.org/reports/eroding-trust-uk-s-prevent-counter-extremism-strategy-health-and-education.

10 Timothy Mitchell, *Colonising Egypt* (Cambridge, 1991)

11 Mitchell, *Colonising Egypt*

12 See, for example, 'Inspectors to question primary school girls who wear hijab', *Guardian* (19 November 2017), https://www.theguardian.com/education/2017/nov/19/school-inspectors-to-question-primary-school-girls-who-wear-hijab.

Daughter of Stories

Nadine Aisha Jassat

For Ma and Aunt

There are stories in my family that go round and round, so much so you could say that they are what we've been raised on. Each family member has their own way of telling them, their own sense of when to pause in the narrative for dramatic effect, each aunt, uncle or cousin believing their version to be the true original. Some of these stories are lengthy – tales reserved for long car trips where the road stretches out before you like an empty page – and some are short, the essence of who a person was, what they meant to the speaker, held in a single line. Perhaps the first tale I ever knew of my paternal grandmother, Ma – a woman to whose stories I would later turn to navigate questions in my life – was one of these short summations. So much of her ethos, and what it meant to be descended from her, could be gleaned from the simple lines my father would repeat to me as a child: 'My mother, Ma, she would always help others in need. Always.'

Looking back now, I can see that the family I grew up in and was shaped by comprised not only the people around me – my parents and siblings in the UK and my close-knit, wider family in Zimbabwe whom we saw once a year – but also the ghost-like legacies of the previous generations of women in my family. And there were no two greater figures in my childhood stories than my grandmother, Ma (Fatima), and her sister, Aunt (Aisha). The bedtime stories I was raised on were not of blonde princesses, waiting for a man to save them, but of Ma and Aunt: two resourceful and resilient Muslim matriarchs from whom I was descended. Both Ma and Aunt died when I was young, but they remained forever present in the stories passed around my family like lore. And they, too, had passed down stories themselves – of their mother, Mariam, and of their own adventures as Muslim women of mixed heritage growing up in Zimbabwe (which, at the time, still bore the colonial name of Rhodesia, a name which rarely featured in our family stories, unless to highlight injustice). Indeed, if you were to ask me what family means, there might be a whole host of different answers I could give you, some difficult, some wonderful. Without a doubt, one of them would be the sense of settling at my auntie's or father's or cousin's knee, ready to hear a tale of Ma and Aunt, whose stories ruled our family.

In their absence, Ma and Aunt's presence was magnified. It was perhaps through the sharing of their stories, the way each member of my family revered them, that I began to understand the connection between storytelling and isolation, even grief. Sometimes, speaking someone's story is the only way to keep them with you. When my father told my brothers and me stories about Ma and Aunt, he was also telling us about Zimbabwe, about what it meant to be Muslim, about family, about a whole other life and way of being which existed across the gulf between the UK and Zimbabwe. And, in turn, when Ma and Aunt had spoken stories to my father as a child, of their mother, of their lives, they were also passing down knowledge and truths which – under oppressive colonial rule – were too often left unspoken.

My father grew up in a society marked by racial segregation, a separation which was often referred to as the 'colour bar'; a system which, like the apartheid system in neighbouring South Africa, sought to separate people down strict racial lines. Under this, my father and his family were deemed to belong to the category of 'Indian', as this box was seen to be the closest fit of the four options laid out by white colonial rule; the other categories being 'White', 'Black' and 'Coloured'. While part of my father's heritage was indeed Indian, other parts of it were not; Ma and Aunt's mother Mariam, my great-grandmother, was (we are told) the daughter of an African woman and a Christian missionary from Scotland. Mariam was raised in a mission school, and converted to Islam upon marrying her husband, who was Arab and had migrated to Zimbabwe via India at the turn of the century. My paternal grandfather also had mixed heritage: Malay, European and Indian. This diverse history risked being rendered totally invisible under Zimbabwe's strict racial classifications, each category coming with its own permissions and restrictions – *you can go here, you can't go there, you can speak to these people, you can't speak to those*. Amid this rule of silencing of both voice and self, what bonded my family not only to each other but also to a wider community was Islam, and stories.

Spearheaded by Ma and Aunt, Islam gave my family a shared identity of faith and understanding, as well as heritage, belonging and cultural practices in a society marked by racial divides into which they, like many, didn't easily fit. Stories allowed them to still lay claim to that heritage; they were the vehicle used by my family to ensure that this knowledge was passed down. Indeed, what replaced absences or mistruths in official documentation (which could, in turn, determine what was also left forgotten), were the stories my family told, and the people they kept alive with their words. In a world characterised by its emphasis on separation, Islam and stories helped my family to find connection.

Even to begin to explain my heritage to others, now, to answer the dreaded and too often repeated question from strangers – 'where are you from?' – requires a story. There is no one term for the mix of everything we are, and no simple explanation that can be given for how that mix came to be without also drawing on wider history. And to understand my heritage myself, I must call on stories too. Some of these are available to me; tales of Mariam's strong faith, and saris passed down from woman to woman. Some – because of colonialism and its violent legacy – are not, leaving stories of our ancestors which we will perhaps never know, voices we may never hear.

As a child, my favourite story was The Tale of Ma, Aunt and the Mystery of the Mustard Seeds. It was like my own Nancy Drew thriller, except this story was about two old Zimbabwean-Arab ladies in bright clothing, *dupattas* draped over their shoulders and *chappals* pat-patting on the ground, who always saved the day. Even now, I picture them each with their hair – long, thick and dark – pulled back over their heads in a twist, in the same way I pull mine now each morning, a connection found in the everyday. The story went like this.

*

One bright, sunny morning in Zimbabwe, Aunt made her way to Ma's house, to spend her day like she always did: at the side of her sister, cooking up recipes and plots, swapping prescription medicines and gossip, two partners in crime. But on this day, when she arrived at her sister's front door – guarded by a white trellised metal gate – Aunt found something very disturbing. On the front step, left there with a purpose almost like an omen, was a thick scattering of mustard seeds. 'Fatima! Fatima!' Aunt called, shaking the metal gate with a loud clack and clang. 'Fatima, someone has been here to wish ill on you!' Ma came running, asking her sister, 'Ahsu' – her pet name for Aunt, her constant companion – 'Ahsu, what is it? What's wrong?' However, as soon as she got to the door and saw the mustard seeds for herself, she knew the situation was grave.

Now what? Someone had clearly come and deliberately spilt these mustard seeds on the doorstep of their house. The unexplained arrival of so many mustard seeds was no small thing – they could only have been left there by someone who intended to jinx Ma and her family. But that someone clearly didn't know who they were dealing with.

And so, the sisters called a taxi – always Rixi Taxis – and instructed the driver to take them all around Harare, in search of a faith healer who could cleanse and bless the home, and dispel the evil. How they did this varies between the different versions of the story; in some versions they had to visit three different places, with one man demanding gold, one demanding silver, and one demanding a goat. In other versions, it was a peaceful *dua* that was recommended, to bring life back into harmony. For the purposes of the story, how they sought to dispel the evil was not important (and indeed, it was later discovered that the mustard seeds had been accidentally spilt by an errant daughter-in-law who – observing the dramatic proceedings – hadn't felt able to own up to the crime). What was important was that no matter what came to one sister's door – whether it was trouble or mustard seeds – the other sister would be there by her side, calling her name, the first to jump into the Rixi beside her, saying through her actions and words, 'If you need me, I am here.'

These were two women I could get behind, and indeed my first knowledge of what it meant to be a Muslim woman was based on these two innovative sisters, always up to one scheme or another, who were as resourceful as they were loving, an unstoppable force.

The Tale of Ma, Aunt and the Mystery of the Mustard Seeds was just one in a fascinating series from which I learned about how to be in the world. Whether it was Ma giving out *duas* from her prayer bag to women in the community who came to her in need, or Aunt's love for Hindi cinema and beautiful possessions, the passion with which they lived their lives followed them in the tales that were their legacy. In the stories of Ma and Aunt I found magic and warmth and adventure. They were cheeky and superstitious and complex, but above all they were brave. Hearing the stories of Ma and Aunt, I would go to bed each night dreaming of the adventurers in my blood, connected to a legacy that felt special, and filled me with pride. I would need that pride to counter-balance the steady tide of discrimination, misunderstanding and prejudice which circled the shore of my childhood like waves, and left its mark in the sand, which only kind words and family hands could help smooth away.

My realization that I was different – that I was seen as something other, something new – began in the playground, if not long before. Growing up in the UK there were boxes – no longer the same rigid institution of the 'colour bar', but still there – that my family and I didn't fit into. My father is brown and Muslim, my mother white and Christian. If, as a child, you consider your luck in life to be drawn by the number of occasions when you get delicious food and presents, then coming from a multi-faith household which celebrated Christmas *and* Eid, I had won the jackpot. Prejudice came from the outside, and my awareness of my difference started at this periphery; questions about where I was from, where my father was from, comments to my parents in the street. Words swirling around me not yet processed, waiting to settle in my mind, on my skin.

One day, a new girl, who was also from a faith community, joined our school. I remember her words as clearly as I remember the check pattern on my school dress, the small buttons in the shape of daisies, and the heavy feeling in my heart which followed. 'What are you?' she asked, while other children skipped over ropes and hopped between chalk lines, the playground alive around us. 'My mum's Christian, and my dad's Muslim,' I replied, hoping in my childhood naivety for solidarity, an understanding, a bond, maybe a friend. 'You can't be both Muslim *and* Christian,' she replied. 'You can't be *nothing*.' And there, aged seven years old, I was suddenly speechless for the first time. Her words seemed to take mine away, and I was no longer sure who I was. I found myself faced with the idea that by existing outside the lines of established communities, I either had to abandon myself and choose to be a part of only one, or be 'nothing', be non-existent, be alone.

It's interesting that this is a moment I return to even now – because it reminds me that I must try to rewrite my voice into experiences where I was left voiceless, try to redress the balance and make peace with the past. But the past and its categories do not always stay there, and as I grew I found a disconnect, a rift, between my identity – the one I defined for myself as a woman from a mixed and multi-faith background – and the one others expected of me, the boxes they had in mind. Depending on the context, I was often deemed by other people to be either 'too Muslim' or 'not Muslim enough', 'too secular' or 'not secular enough', 'too brown' or 'not brown enough', 'too white' or 'not white enough'. I felt as if I had been unwittingly placed in the middle of a tug of war, and was trying desperately to hold on to myself. The more one side pulled, the more I began to feel separated from the other. My identity seemed constantly up for negotiation by everyone else but me, as if I were forever trying to navigate an in-between space into which others projected their questions about my body, my family, my beliefs: *Do you follow after your mother or father? Why do you have your mother's face, but your father's colouring? Why does your hair look like that? Are your parents still together? Are you Muslim or Christian? Are you nothing?*

I had been raised to identify as a Muslim, but as an adult I didn't practise. I had developed – like many people both inside and outside Islam – my own sense of spirituality which felt unique and personal to me. However, I still knew that Islam was a thread running through my identity, woven within like the many lessons and experiences that had shaped me and my life. It was present in my family, in familiar and shared practices; it was at the heart of many of my key values and frames of reference. Islam is a part of who I am, a part of my story. Consequently, to be told by others that I was 'not Muslim enough', or that my existence lingered dangerously over a 'nothing' I couldn't be, felt as if I was being pushed directly into that nothing, denying not only my existence, but also my connection to my family, my heritage, and my story.

Family storytelling, then, was an antidote to this dismissal – a way of preserving my heritage in a world where that connection was constantly challenged. For it seems clear to me that many of the connections to Islam which I hold most dear today – giving *zakat*, cherishing blessings and prayers on my tongue, *mashallah, inshallah, alhamdulillah* – are the ones I gained from family: an inheritance of whispered words held like muscle memory; the fact that 'I love you' is only the first half of the sentence, always completed with the words 'may Allah bless and keep you'; and the remembrance of Ma, a woman who gave and helped those in need, always. Simply put, stories of Ma helped me to understand Islam, and Islam helped me to understand Ma, her values, her life, what she lived by. I cannot unpick my sense of who I am in relation to Islam from the thread of being a part of Ma, Aunt and my wider family. Even my name, the Aisha which sits proudly in the middle, proclaims not only my connection to the faith so close to my heart, but also to Aunt, the Aisha who came before me, the heroine of so many of my favourite family tales. Even in my name there is a story.

My name, and the story present in it, was just one of many beacons which I held on to in my determination to keep other people's judgements at bay. I am a young, mixed woman, and have grown up with racism on one shoulder and sexism on the other. At one time in my life it felt as though not a week went by without a stranger commenting on my appearance, either asking me where I was from or telling me, violently, what they thought of my body, what they'd like to do to it. When you are spoken over, spoken for, or denied a voice – as I was, every time a car zoomed past with men shouting sexist taunts without giving me a chance to answer, every time I was told to take being asked where I was from as a compliment, not to mention further stories beyond these pages – then storytelling becomes the ultimate tool of resistance. For when my father told me stories of Ma and Aunt to keep alive a sense of our heritage and roots, he was also teaching me how to exist and thrive like them; caring for others, seeking to right wrongs, maintaining solidarity, and sticking to my convictions. Perhaps unknowingly, he also helped armour my tongue, passing on key principles which now underpin my own writing and storytelling. Ma's care for community, Aunt's loyalty and ferocity, were not simply lessons in family history, but lessons in how to endure, how to meet whatever challenges may come to your door. These stories were tools of resilience and survival, and they helped me navigate climates of prejudice and challenge by drawing on the strength and lessons from those gone before.

I wonder what would have happened to me, had I not had those stories. I often find myself considering the impact of a lack of stories celebrating women like Ma and Aunt – Muslim women, mixed women, cheeky, entrepreneurial, brave women – not only in our homes, but also out in the world. I work as a creative practitioner, exploring social justice issues with young people, using creative methods like storytelling, drama and writing to help open up conversations around inequality and change. In the discussions that take place in this context, particularly with young women of colour and young women of Muslim heritage, it quickly becomes apparent that the consequences of the lack of these stories are still being felt, whether in playgrounds, newspapers or the national media. Time and again, the young women I hear from are quick to draw attention to the lack of representation of the history and achievements of Muslim women and women of colour in the education they receive, the media they are exposed to, and the stories they and their peers hear. They are often then quick to link this lack of positive representation with the discrimination they experience at school or out in the street, not to mention on a structural, institutional and political level.

This dynamic – between whose stories are told, and by whom, and who is respected or who is targeted – is played out across society. For is there not a connection between silence and oppression, a space where prejudice can flourish, and storytelling and liberation, a space where words and truth can move towards change? In a society where racism, Islamophobia and misogyny are present, it makes it that much harder for those who experience multiple oppressions to be heard. When we are heard, however, it has the potential to open up avenues of opportunity for connection and change. But, if you cannot find stories about those like you in the first place, or when the stories you are told about those like you are harmful and limiting – not filled with joy and pride like the tales of Ma and Aunt were for me – it can make it difficult to speak in the first place, whether out of a fear of how others may react, or fear that you, as the speaker, won't be listened to. There are so many tales missing in the world; consequently we need more storytellers to tell them. No one woman can speak for all

Muslim women – for that rich and varied tapestry of experiences, practice, belief and ways of being. We need as many stories and storytellers as there are people, a greater cacophony of diverse voices and views, and listeners who welcome them.

That fellow schoolgirl I encountered in the playground all those years ago told me I couldn't be 'nothing' because my existence was a story which she had never been told. It was a gap her imagination could not fill. Perhaps it is no surprise, then, that my path in life led me to becoming a writer and a poet, who draws on lived experience to explore issues of inequality, as well as my creative practice and work with marginalized groups – groups whose stories are often ignored or silenced – to invest in their voices growing, thriving, speaking out.

In the same way that Ma and Aunt jumped in a Rixi in search of a solution to their challenge, I turned to storytelling as a way to regain my voice against experiences of voicelessness; to push back against currents that tried to define me incorrectly, by defining me for myself instead. Up until that point, experiences of prejudice, violence and silencing had been dropped in a steady stream like mustard seeds at my door, growing heavier and heavier each day. Storytelling, writing, truth-telling, has been my way of sweeping these mustard seeds away. My method of resistance to those who would say that I, and people like me, are 'too much' or 'not enough' or 'nothing', has been to write myself and my experiences into existence, with honesty and with stories that are mine, a precise blend of all my different threads.

Whenever Ma and Aunt encountered injustice, whether it was Aunt finding mustard seeds at Ma's door, or Ma counselling women in her community with her prayer bag, they used what resources they had available to them to try and help. Ma and Aunt were sisters, and they were fighters. They looked out for each other. And I am their granddaughter, the daughter of storytellers, the daughter of stories. I carry the legacy they left to me, the one that asks me to use the power that I have – my voice, my pen, my words – to try and continue to sweep the mustard seeds of injustice and oppression away. To share strength and solidarity and stories. In doing so, in embracing storytelling, I am able to embrace not only my unique identity, but also to stay connected to theirs. I am able to keep them by my side, their hands as close to mine while I write as the jewellery they once wore, gold circling my fingers and wrists, their laughter and antics present in my stories, in the ethos which underpins my work. From a child sitting on a family member's knee to an adult writing these words today, storytelling has helped me to realize and reaffirm who I am. And should I ever doubt, or need a reminder, then all I have to do is turn to these pages, and remember the stories of two women, dark hair braided like crowns, *chappals* pat-patting and scarves blowing behind them like capes as they stride off on another adventure, ready to save the day.

Contributor Biographies

Mona Eltahawy is an award-winning columnist and international public speaker on Arab and Muslim issues and global feminism. She is the author of *Headscarves and Hymens: Why the Middle East Needs a Sexual Revolution*, is a contributor to the *New York Times* opinion pages and is a regular guest analyst on various television and radio shows. In November 2011, Egyptian riot police beat her, breaking her left arm and right hand, and sexually assaulted her. She was detained for twelve hours by the Interior Ministry and Military Intelligence. *Newsweek* magazine named her one of its '150 Fearless Women of 2012', *Time* magazine featured her along with other activists from around the world in its 'People of the Year' and *Arabian Business* magazine named her one of the '100 Most Powerful Arab Women'. She is based in Cairo and New York City.

Coco Khan is a journalist for the *Guardian*. She is also a regular contributor to the *Independent* and *New York Magazine*, among others, and is editor-at-large with youth publication, *Complex*. Her essay, 'Whose Voice Is It Anyway?: Ethnicity and Authenticity in the Arts', appeared in *Counterculture UK* in 2015. Most recently, her short fictional memoir, 'Flags', featured in *The Good Immigrant* (2016), and won praise from the *Spectator*, *Vice* and the BBC. The piece was subsequently adapted for BBC Radio 4's Book of the Week. Coco writes a weekly column in the *Guardian Weekend*. She was born and raised in London.

Sufiya Ahmed is the award-winning author of the Young Adult novel *Secrets of the Henna Girl*, published by Puffin Book, and a public speaker on girls' rights. Sufiya regularly visits secondary schools to deliver author sessions and writing workshops. She also discusses her previous career in the Houses of Parliament to educate and inspire pupils about the democratic process. Sufiya is the founder and director of the BIBI Foundation, a non-profit organization which arranges visits to the Houses of Parliament for diverse and underprivileged children. She regularly contributes to the *Huffington Post* and the *Independent*.

Nafisa Bakkar is one of the co-founders of Amaliah. com. She was named by Forbes as one of ten entrepreneurs under thirty to watch and has been featured in CNN, the *Metro* and *Wired*. Amaliah is an online publisher that creates culturally relevant content for and by Muslim women. With over 100 contributors covering fashion, beauty and world events, Amaliah spotlights the real voices of Muslim women – their work seeks to document, celebrate and challenge Muslim culture while pushing for positive cultural change.

Afia Ahmed is a teacher, writer and researcher based in London. She graduated with a degree in BA History, gained her Master's in Education Policy at King's College London, and is currently working towards her PGDE at UCL's IoE. She is an avid reader, highly enjoys her morning cups of coffee, and can be found entertaining her daughter in the corner of a children's library. Her areas of interests include religion, education, and social mobility.

Yassmin Midhat Abdel-Magied is a Sudanese-born Australian mechanical engineer, writer, broadcaster and award-winning social advocate. She is the author of a memoir, *Yassmin's Story*, and a young adult novel, *You Must Be Layla*. Her words can be found in *Teen Vogue*, the *New York Times*, the *Guardian* and numerous anthologies.

Jamilla Hekmoun is a London-based researcher. She is an avid mental health advocate and volunteers for mental health charities. She has a BA in Arabic and Middle East Studies from the University of Exeter and an MA in Islam in Contemporary Britain from Cardiff University.

Afshan D'souza-Lodhi was born in Dubai and is of Indian/Pakistani descent. Afshan is a writer and performer. She writes plays, prose and performance pieces. She has completed residencies at Royal Exchange Theatre, Manchester Literature Festival and has worked with Eclipse Theatre, Tamasha Theatre Company and Paul Burston's Polari. Afshan is currently Editor in Chief of *TCS* and sits on the board of Brighter Sound. Follow Afshan on twitter @ashlodhi or visit her website, www.afshan.info.

Salma Haidrani is a multi-award-winning writer and journalist ('Young Journalist of the Year' at the GG2

Leadership Awards 2017). Her work predominantly focuses on women's rights, marginalized communities, contemporary faith and social issues, and she has appeared on UK TV and radio, including BBC Radio 4 and Sky News. She writes for magazines and websites including *Vice*, *Cosmopolitan*, *Stylist* and *The Pool*.

Amna Saleem is a Scottish Pakistani comedy writer and broadcaster living between Glasgow and California. Her first sitcom came out in August 2019 and she has a young adult novel expected in the near future. Amna can be found in national publications such as the *Guardian*, *BBC News*, the *New Statesmen* and *Glamour* where she tackles topics such as race, mental health and pop culture. As a broadcaster she has been featured on the BBC, Sky and ITV among others. She thinks feminism is good and racism is bad. Her parents are still waiting for her to get a real job. She is on Twitter @AGlasgowGirl where she regularly overshares and fights bigots.

Saima Mir is an award-winning journalist. A recipient of the Commonwealth Broadcast Association World View Award, Saima has written for *The Times*, the *Guardian*, and the *Independent*. She was also a journalist for the BBC. Her first novel was longlisted for the Bath Novel Award and the SI Leeds Literary Prize. Saima is currently working on her new book.

Born in Egypt and raised in the North of England, **Salma El-Wardany** returned to Cairo just in time for the Arab Spring. Between protesting and fighting in the revolution, she started a blog to document her experiences in Cairo while discussing ideas of womanhood and how gender identities manifest in today's world.

Since returning from Egypt, she has worked with Edinburgh University on the Dangerous Woman Project, given a TEDx Talk, writes for the *HuffPost* as well as various other magazines, is working on her debut novel *Burkas & Bikinis* and performs her poetry across the US and UK, and on BBC radio, while also running an international business. You can find her drinking tea, fighting for a new narrative around Muslims, eating cake and dressing down the patriarchy at every available opportunity.

Aina Khan is a London lawyer who has specialized in family law for over twenty-five years. Her London law firm, Aina Khan Law, focuses on complex and international cases, and she is a world-renowned expert on Islamic family law. Aina started the 'Register Our Marriage' campaign (www.registerourmarriage.org) in 2014. She has travelled across the UK to spread the message that unregistered religious marriages mean no legal rights. Aina was awarded an OBE in 2018 for 'Services to the Protection of Women and Children in Unregistered Marriages'. www.ainakhan.com

Raifa Rafiq is a writer and trainee solicitor at one of the leading international law firms in the UK. She is also the creator and co-host of the literature and popular culture podcast Mostly Lit, named by the *Guardian* and the BBC as one of the top podcasts of 2017. In 2018, the *Bookseller*, selected Mostly Lit as part of its FutureBook40, a list of forty game-changers and innovators within the publishing industry, and Mostly Lit won Podcast of the Year at the FutureBook Awards. Raifa has appeared at Cheltenham Literature Festival, and interviewed authors for BBC Sunday Morning Live and

Waterstones. She has written for the *Guardian*, *Stylist*, Media Diversified, gal-dem and Amaliah, and often shares her thoughts online, reflecting pride in her identity as a Black Muslim woman.

Malia Bouattia is the former president of the National Union of Students (NUS), elected at the National Conference in April 2016. She was the first female Black British and Muslim leader of the NUS.

Nadine Aisha Jassat is a poet, writer and creative practitioner who has been published online, in film and in print. Her work has drawn great acclaim; including receiving a New Writers' Award from the Scottish Book Trust, and being shortlisted for the prestigious Edwin Morgan Poetry Award. As a creative practitioner, she has delivered significant education and creative participation work, and she was named as one of '30 Inspiring Young Women Under 30' by YWCA Scotland. Her debut poetry collection, *Let Me Tell You This*, is released in March 2019 with award-winning publisher 404 Ink.

Acknowledgements

Praise be to Allah, for this opportunity and this platform.

Thank you to every contributor who shared their essay in this book.

Thank you to Nikesh Shukla, Wei Ming-Kam and Louie Stowell; without you, this book wouldn't exist. You believed in me and have been the kindest friends and I am grateful for your support. To Daniel Huw Bowen, Rachel Faturoti, Anthony Lee and Ammara Isa, thank you for all the pep talks, for never letting me waver and encouraging me to be brave.

To my agent Molly Ker-Hawn, thank you for believing in this book and always offering me a listening ear.

Thank you to my editor Sophie Jonathan, for taking a chance on me, for your enthusiasm from the beginning, for your kindness and for understanding the importance of this book.

Thank you to my family for all their support and patience.